easy vegetarian dinners

GRAND
AVENUE
BOOKS

Grand Avenue Books

An imprint of Meredith® Corporation

Easy Vegetarian Dinners

Contributing Editors: Sharyl Heiken, Rosemary Hutchinson
   (Spectrum Communication Services)

Contributing Designer: Joline Rivera

Copy and Production Editor: Victoria Forlini

Copy Chief: Terri Fredrickson

Contributing Proofreaders: Jane Carlson, Susan J. Kling, Beth Lastine

Editorial Operations Manager: Karen Schirm

Manager, Book Production: Rick von Holdt

Editorial and Design Assistants: Karen McFadden, Mary Lee Gavin, Patricia Loder

Grand Avenue Books

Editor In Chief: Linda Raglan Cunningham

Design Director: Matt Strelecki

Executive Editor, Grand Avenue Books: Dan Rosenberg

Publisher: James D. Blume

Executive Director, Marketing: Jeffrey Myers

Executive Director, New Business Development: Todd M. Davis

Executive Director, Sales: Ken Zagor

Director, Operations: George A. Susral

Director, Production: Douglas M. Johnston

Business Director: Jim Leonard

Vice President and General Manager: Douglas J. Guendel

Meredith Publishing Group

President, Publishing Group: Stephen M. Lacy

Vice President-Publishing Director: Bob Mate

Meredith Corporation

Chairman and Chief Executive Officer: William T. Kerr

In Memoriam: E.T. Meredith III (1933-2003)

All of us at Grand Avenue Books are dedicated to providing you with the information and ideas you need to create delicious foods. We welcome your comments and suggestions. Write to us at: Grand Avenue Books, Editorial Department LN-114, 1716 Locust Street, Des Moines, IA 50309-3023

Pictured on front cover: Sautéed Onion and Tomato Sandwiches (see recipe, page 209)

MEATLESS MEALS

Look at everything from trendy restaurant menus to college dormitory steam tables to office sack lunches, and you'll notice that more and more Americans enjoy meatless meals. The reasons are many, but one of the top ones is that the eye-popping variety of protein-rich grains, beans, vegetables, and fruits available makes meatless cooking delicious and fun.

No matter whether your family has already discovered vegetarian dining or you're trying it for the first time, *Easy Vegetarian Dinners* offers you inspiration. With more than 100 extraordinary recipes and practical hints for working meatless dishes into your family's routine, you'll have just what you need for terrific vegetarian meals.

Most of these full-flavored meatless recipes are ready in 30 minutes or less and start with everyday ingredients. To make the most of grains, beans, and vegetables, there's Mixed Bean and Portobello Ragout, Southwestern Black Bean Cakes with Guacamole, Hoppin' John Vegetable Pilaf, and more. If you're partial to pasta, try dishes such as Teriyaki Penne, Lemony Alfredo-Style Fettuccine, or Cheese Tortellini with Cannellini Bean Sauce. When it comes to soup, simmer the likes of Hearty Bean and Rice Soup, Corn and Green Chile Chowder, or Tunisian Vegetable Chili. For a quick salad, sandwich, or pizza, opt for Middle Eastern Bulgur-Spinach Salad, Eggplant Panini, Falafel Burgers in Pitas, or Grilled Sicilian-Style Pizza. And when you want to enjoy eggs and cheese, prepare Spinach and Cheese Omelet, Asparagus-Potato Scramble, or Mushroom and Pepper Frittata.

Sample the captivating recipes from *Easy Vegetarian Dinners* and you'll be convinced that cooking meatless—either every day or just once in a while—can be one of the most satisfying ways to feed your family.

Polenta with Portobello Sauce
(see recipe, page 130)

HEATHFUL EATING—VEGETARIAN STYLE

Whether you enjoy an occasional meatless meal or have become completely vegetarian, cooking with grains, beans, and vegetables is easier and more delicious than ever.

Including vegetarian dishes in your diet is a great way to add variety and interest to meals and may provide some significant health benefits. Whether you're an old pro at cooking meatless or are just getting started, here are some helpful facts about the world of vegetarian dining.

Is a Vegetarian Diet Healthful?

Most health experts agree that following a low-fat diet that's high in fiber and rich in vitamins and minerals is the nutritious way to go. A vegetarian diet that relies heavily on a well-balanced assortment of legumes, grains, vegetables, and fruits can provide you with the nutrients and fiber you need. What's more, some of these foods contain phytochemicals (for example beta carotene and isoflavone genistein)—compounds that are believed to help reduce the risk of heart disease and cancer.

Following a meatless diet doesn't automatically guarantee that you're eating healthfully. As with any health-smart meal plan, it's important to keep the amount of fat and cholesterol low in the vegetarian dishes you eat and to make sure your meals include a variety of foods that provide enough calories, protein, and a good mix of vitamins and minerals.

Guide to a Balanced Vegetarian Diet

Here are some handy rules of thumb to help you plan nutritious, well-balanced meatless meals for the day.

• Put the emphasis on eating a variety of legumes (beans, peas, and lentils), whole grains, vegetables, and fruits. Eat more of these items than other foods. Use dairy products, eggs, nuts, seeds, fat, oils, and sweeteners in moderation. Grains and cereals such as wheat, corn, oats, and rice contribute a good supply of protein to the diet. And grains also provide fiber, carbohydrates, B vitamins, and iron. Vegetables and fruits provide fiber, vitamins, and minerals.

• Choose at least two servings of low-fat or fat-free, high-calcium foods daily. Including dairy products in your diet is the best way to make sure you get enough calcium. If you'd rather not eat dairy products, eating other high-calcium foods is essential. Some options include calcium-fortified soy milk or orange juice, tofu processed with calcium sulfate, and green leafy vegetables.

• Include 2 to 3 servings of meat substitutes in your meals each day. Select from dried beans, nuts, seeds, peanut butter or other nut butters, or eggs. Soy products are other good sources of protein. Look for tofu, tempeh, veggie burgers, soy milk, and soy cheese or ice cream at the store. Contrary to what was advised in the past, it's not necessary to mix and match proteins as long as you eat a variety each day.

• In addition to calcium, there are several nutrients that are likely to be lacking in a vegetarian diet. Keep these nutrients in mind and try to eat some of the following suggested foods each day.

Vitamin B$_{12}$: This vitamin is usually not a problem if you eat dairy products and eggs, If you don't, try to eat vitamin B$_{12}$-fortified breakfast cereals, soymilk products, or vegetarian burgers.

Vitamin D: Milk is naturally high in vitamin D. If you don't want to drink milk, opt for fortified breakfast cereals and fortified soy beverages.

Iron: Foods rich in iron include legumes (beans, lentils, and peas), dark-green leafy vegetables (such as spinach or kale), iron-fortified cereals and breads, whole-grain products, seeds, prune juice, dried fruit, and black-strap molasses.

Zinc: Good sources of zinc include whole grains (especially the germ and bran), whole wheat bread, legumes (beans, lentils, and peas), tofu, seeds (including sesame seeds, pumpkin seeds, and sunflower kernels), and nuts.

• Team vitamin C-rich foods such as citrus fruits, melons, sweet peppers, and broccoli with iron-rich foods such as beans. This will help your body absorb iron more efficiently.

• If there are children in your family, it's especially important to plan ahead. Because vegetarian meals are often low in fat and high in fiber, they may not provide youngsters with the calories and nutrients they need. Make sure your children eat at least some higher-calorie foods with more fat. Items such as peanut butter, nuts, and cheese are ideal. And encourage them to eat several snacks throughout the day to provide both calories and nutrients. Also, check with a registered dietitian, doctor, or pediatric nurse about recommendations for nutritional supplements. Vitamin B$_{12}$, vitamin D, calcium, iron, and zinc are the nutrients of particular concern.

Meatless Dining for the Family

It may take your family a little time to learn to enjoy meatless meals, so it's best to introduce them gradually. Here are some suggestions for helping to make meatless meals a hit.

• Start with the meatless dishes your family already enjoys—for example, pasta primavera, spaghetti with marinara sauce, or vegetable soup. Keep these favorites on the menu while you gradually add new dishes.

• Surround a new vegetarian entrée with side dishes you know your family likes. For example, team vegetarian stew with garlic bread, a tossed salad, and ice cream.

• Choose one day a week to eat meatless. This way everyone knows what to expect on "meatless day." Or if an entire day is too much, try going meatless a meal at a time. Then slowly increase the number of vegetarian meals.

• Explore ethnic dishes. Try Mexican bean burritos or vegetable fajitas, Chinese fried rice, Middle Eastern tabbouleh, or Italian minestrone.

• Rely on dried beans and legumes. There's a huge variety to choose from with different tastes and textures. You can use them in casseroles, soups, salads, dips, salsas, and sauces. Try lima beans one night and black beans another. Or experiment by adding a new kind of bean to your trademark chili or soup.

• Switch breakfast foods to dinner time. French toast, waffles, and omelets can all make a great supper.

• Substitute tofu for beef or chicken in stir-fries, pasta casseroles, or soups.

• Revamp pizza by replacing pepperoni or sausage with a medley of favorite vegetables, such as red onions; red, yellow, or green sweet peppers; mushrooms; dried or fresh tomatoes; and artichoke hearts. Or dress up an unbaked cheese pizza from the supermarket with sautéed sweet peppers, broccoli, leeks, or zucchini.

• Check the frozen food section or refrigerator case at the supermarket for cheese- or vegetable-filled pastas, such as ravioli, cannelloni, or tortellini. Or look at the latest array of soy or texturized-protein products including burgers, sausagelike crumbles, and meatlike balls.

• For quick suppers, rely on packaged grain and rice mixes. If you like, make them a bit heartier by stirring in canned beans, nuts, or tofu.

• Expand your snack horizons by trying new combinations. How about cashew butter on rice cakes? Or baked tortilla chips with bean dip?

EGGS & CHEESE

From frittatas to quesadillas, these egg and cheese specialties are hearty and satisfying.

Mushroom and Pepper Frittata
(see recipe, page 24)

EGG RAGOUT

Keep this recipe handy for those times when your supermarket gets in a good supply of baby squash. Or substitute 1 cup cubed zucchini or yellow summer squash.

Start to Finish: 25 minutes **Makes:** 4 servings

1½ cups fresh sugar snap peas, strings and tips removed

1 cup baby sunburst squash, cut into quarters

4 green onions, thinly bias-sliced

4 teaspoons margarine or butter

2 tablespoons all-purpose flour

1¼ cups milk

2 tablespoons grated Parmesan cheese

1 teaspoon sweet-hot mustard or Dijon-style mustard

4 hard-cooked eggs, coarsely chopped

4 bagels, split and toasted, or 4 slices whole wheat bread, toasted

1

In a covered medium saucepan cook sugar snap peas and squash in a small amount of boiling salted water for 2 to 4 minutes or until vegetables are crisp-tender; drain.

2

For sauce, in a large saucepan cook green onions in hot margarine or butter over medium heat until tender. Stir in flour. Add milk all at once. Cook and stir until thickened and bubbly. Stir in Parmesan cheese and mustard; add cooked vegetables. Cook and stir about 1 minute more or until heated through. Gently stir in eggs.

3

To serve, spoon egg mixture over bagels or toasted bread.

Nutrition Facts per serving: 392 calories, 13 g total fat, 221 mg cholesterol, 600 mg sodium, 49 g carbohydrate, 19 g protein.

FRENCH OMELET

Whether you opt for it plain or filled with mushrooms, cheese, or fruit, this tender omelet is a delicious choice for breakfast, brunch, or supper.

Start to Finish: 10 minutes **Makes:** 1 serving

2 **eggs**
1 **tablespoon water**
⅛ **teaspoon salt**

Dash ground black pepper
Nonstick cooking spray

1

In a small bowl use a fork to beat together the eggs, the water, salt, and pepper until combined but not frothy. Coat an unheated 8- or 10-inch nonstick skillet with flared sides with nonstick cooking spray. Preheat over medium heat.

2

Add egg mixture to skillet. As eggs set, run a spatula around the edge of the skillet, lifting eggs so uncooked portion flows underneath. When eggs are set but still glossy and moist, remove from the heat. Fold omelet in half. Transfer to a warm plate.

Nutrition Facts per serving: 149 calories, 10 g total fat, 425 mg cholesterol, 417 mg sodium, 1 g carbohydrate, 13 g protein.

Mushroom Omelet: Prepare French Omelet as directed, except for filling, cook ⅓ cup sliced fresh mushrooms in 1 tablespoon hot margarine or butter until tender. When eggs are set but still glossy and moist, spoon filling across center of omelet. Fold sides of omelet over filling.

Nutrition Facts per serving: 259 calories, 22 g total fat, 425 mg cholesterol, 552 mg sodium, 2 g carbohydrate, 14 g protein.

Cheese Omelet: Prepare French Omelet as directed, except omit salt. When eggs are set but still glossy and moist, sprinkle ¼ cup shredded cheddar, Swiss, or Monterey Jack cheese across center of omelet. Fold sides of omelet over cheese.

Nutrition Facts per serving: 263 calories, 19 g total fat, 455 mg cholesterol, 302 mg sodium, 2 g carbohydrate, 20 g protein.

Fruit Omelet: Prepare French Omelet as directed, except omit pepper. When eggs are set but still glossy and moist, spread 2 tablespoons dairy sour cream or yogurt across center of omelet. Fold sides of omelet over sour cream. Top with ¼ cup halved fresh strawberries; sliced, peeled peaches; or blueberries. Sprinkle with 1 tablespoon brown sugar.

Nutrition Facts per serving: 263 calories, 15 g total fat, 436 mg cholesterol, 436 mg sodium, 18 g carbohydrate, 13 g protein.

SPINACH AND CHEESE OMELET

For a lower-fat, lower-cholesterol omelet, use the egg product option and substitute reduced-fat cheddar cheese for the regular cheddar.

Start to Finish: 20 minutes **Makes:** 2 servings

²/₃ cup chopped red sweet pepper

2 tablespoons finely chopped onion

1 tablespoon cider vinegar

¼ teaspoon ground black pepper

4 eggs or 1 cup refrigerated or frozen
   egg product, thawed

Dash salt

Dash ground red pepper

Nonstick cooking spray

¼ cup shredded sharp cheddar cheese
   (1 ounce)

1 tablespoon snipped fresh chives,
   fresh flat-leaf parsley, or fresh
   chervil

1 cup fresh spinach leaves

1

For the red pepper relish, in a small bowl combine sweet pepper, onion, vinegar, and black pepper. Set aside.

2

In a large bowl use a rotary beater or wire whisk to beat together the eggs, salt, and ground red pepper until frothy. Coat an unheated 8-inch nonstick skillet with flared sides or a crepe pan with nonstick cooking spray. Preheat skillet over medium heat. Pour egg mixture into the prepared skillet. As eggs set, run a spatula around edge of the skillet, lifting eggs so uncooked portion flows underneath.

3

When eggs are set but still glossy and moist, sprinkle with cheese and chives, parsley, or chervil. Top with ³/₄ cup of the spinach and 2 tablespoons of the red pepper relish. Fold 1 side of omelet over filling. Top with the remaining spinach and 1 tablespoon of the red pepper relish. (Store the remaining red pepper relish in the refrigerator for up to 3 days. Use on sandwiches or omelets.)

4

To serve, cut the omelet in half. Transfer to 2 dinner plates.

Nutrition Facts per serving: 214 calories, 15 g total fat, 440 mg cholesterol, 303 mg sodium, 3 g carbohydrate, 17 g protein.

ASPARAGUS-POTATO SCRAMBLE

To quickly thaw the hash brown potatoes and asparagus, run them under cool running water.

Start to Finish: 20 minutes **Makes:** 5 servings

Nonstick cooking spray

2 cups loose-pack frozen diced hash brown potatoes with onions and sweet peppers, thawed

2 tablespoons sliced green onion

6 beaten egg whites

3 beaten eggs

3 tablespoons fat-free milk

1 tablespoon snipped fresh basil or $1/2$ teaspoon dried basil, crushed

$1/8$ teaspoon salt

$1/8$ teaspoon ground black pepper

1 pound fresh asparagus, cut into 1-inch pieces ($1^1/2$ cups) or one 10-ounce package frozen cut asparagus, thawed and well drained

$1/4$ cup shredded reduced-fat sharp cheddar cheese (1 ounce)

1

Generously coat an unheated large nonstick skillet with nonstick cooking spray. Preheat over medium heat. Add hash brown potatoes and green onion; cook for 4 to 5 minutes or until ingredients begin to brown.

2

Meanwhile, in a large bowl use a rotary beater or wire whisk to beat together egg whites, whole eggs, milk, basil, salt, and black pepper. Stir in asparagus. Pour egg mixture over potatoes and green onion. Cook, without stirring, until mixture begins to set on the bottom and around edge. Using a spatula or a large spoon, lift and fold the partially cooked egg mixture so the uncooked portion flows underneath. Continue cooking and folding about 4 minutes more or until eggs are cooked through but are still glossy and moist.

3

Remove skillet from heat; sprinkle with cheese. Cover and let stand for 1 minute or until cheese is melted.

Nutrition Facts per serving: 184 calories, 9 g total fat, 132 mg cholesterol, 217 mg sodium, 14 g carbohydrate, 12 g protein.

KNIFE-AND-FORK BREAKFAST BURRITO

*For a company brunch, team these Tex-Mex fold-overs with fresh fruit and
toasted French bread or a coffee cake.*

Start to Finish: 25 minutes **Makes:** 4 servings

1 cup canned black beans, rinsed and
  drained
$1/3$ cup bottled chunky salsa
4 slightly beaten eggs
2 tablespoons milk
$1/4$ teaspoon ground black pepper
$1/8$ teaspoon salt
  Nonstick cooking spray or
  cooking oil

12 to 16 thin slices red, yellow, and/or
  green tomato
$1/2$ cup crumbled queso fresco or
  shredded Monterey Jack cheese
  (2 ounces)
$1/4$ cup dairy sour cream
4 teaspoons shredded fresh mint
  Fresh mint leaves (optional)
  Bottled chunky salsa (optional)

1

In a small saucepan mash the beans slightly. Stir in the $1/3$ cup salsa. Heat through over low heat. Cover
and keep warm while making egg tortillas.

2

In a medium bowl use a fork to beat together the eggs, milk, pepper, and salt until combined. Coat an
unheated 10-inch nonstick omelet pan (or skillet with flared sides) with nonstick cooking spray or
brush lightly with a little cooking oil. Preheat pan over medium heat until a drop of water sizzles.

3

For each egg tortilla, pour about $1/4$ cup of the egg mixture into the pan. Lift and tilt pan to spread egg
mixture over bottom. Return to heat. Cook for $1^{1}/2$ to 2 minutes or until lightly browned on bottom (do
not turn). Loosen edge of the egg tortilla with spatula; carefully slide out onto a serving plate,
browned side down.

4

On one half of each egg tortilla, spread some of the bean-salsa mixture. Top with 3 or 4 tomato slices
and about 1 tablespoon of the cheese. Fold in half and then into quarters to form a burrito. Keep warm
while cooking remaining tortillas and assembling burritos.

5

To serve, top with sour cream and remaining cheese; sprinkle with shredded mint. If desired, garnish
with mint leaves and serve with additional salsa.

Nutrition Facts per serving: 185 calories, 9 g total fat, 223 mg cholesterol, 413 mg sodium, 13 g carbohydrate, 12 g protein.

PUFFY OVEN PANCAKE

An herb-seasoned four-vegetable filling transforms a traditional breakfast favorite into a delightful dinner entrée.

Start to Finish: 30 minutes **Makes:** 4 servings

Nonstick cooking spray
2 eggs
2 egg whites
½ cup fat-free milk
½ cup all-purpose flour
⅛ teaspoon salt
1 cup sliced fresh mushrooms
1 cup broccoli florets

½ cup chopped onion
1 medium tomato, chopped
2 tablespoons toasted wheat germ
2 teaspoons snipped fresh thyme or oregano or ¼ teaspoon dried thyme or oregano, crushed
1 tablespoon grated Parmesan cheese

1

Coat an unheated 8-inch ovenproof skillet with nonstick cooking spray. Place in a 450°F oven for 2 minutes. Meanwhile, in a medium bowl use a rotary beater or wire whisk to beat together the eggs and egg whites until combined. Add the milk, flour, and salt. Beat until batter is smooth. Immediately pour into hot skillet. Bake for 18 to 20 minutes or until puffed and browned.

2

Meanwhile, coat an unheated medium saucepan with nonstick cooking spray. Preheat over medium heat. Add mushrooms, broccoli, and onion; cook about 5 minutes or until tender, stirring occasionally. Remove from heat. Toss with tomato, wheat germ, and thyme or oregano.

3

To serve, cut the pancake into quarters. Spoon vegetable mixture over quarters. Sprinkle with the Parmesan cheese.

Nutrition Facts per serving: 158 calories, 4 g total fat, 108 mg cholesterol, 184 mg sodium, 20 g carbohydrate, 11 g protein.

VEGETABLE QUESADILLAS

Set out a selection of toppings for these savory wedges.

Start to Finish: 25 minutes **Makes:** 3 servings

¾ cup finely chopped broccoli
¼ cup shredded carrot
¼ cup sliced green onions
2 tablespoons water
6 6-inch flour tortillas
1 teaspoon cooking oil

1 8-ounce package shredded cheddar
  or Monterey Jack cheese with
  jalapeño peppers (2 cups)
Dairy sour cream (optional)
Bottled salsa (optional)
Slivered pitted ripe olives
  (optional)
Sliced green onions (optional)

1

In a 1-quart microwave-safe casserole combine the broccoli, carrot, the ¼ cup green onions, and the water. Cover and microwave on 100-percent (high) power for 2 to 4 minutes or until vegetables are crisp-tender. Drain.

2

Brush 1 side of each of 3 tortillas with some of the oil. Place, oiled sides down, on a baking sheet. Top with the cheese, vegetable mixture, and the remaining tortillas. Brush tops with the remaining oil. Bake in a 450°F oven about 6 minutes or until lightly browned.

3

To serve, cut each tortilla stack into 4 wedges. If desired, serve with sour cream, salsa, olives, and additional green onions.

Nutrition Facts per serving: 499 calories, 30 g total fat, 80 mg cholesterol, 728 mg sodium, 32 g carbohydrate, 24 g protein.

MUSHROOM AND PEPPER FRITTATA

Onion, sweet pepper, and shiitake mushrooms fill this easy frittata with fresh-from-the-garden flavor. (Pictured on page 9.)

Start to Finish: 30 minutes   **Makes:** 4 servings

1 tablespoon cooking oil	1/4 cup fresh basil leaves, sliced into thin strips
1 medium onion, chopped	1/4 cup water
1 red sweet pepper, chopped	1/4 teaspoon salt
8 ounces fresh shiitake mushrooms, sliced	1/4 teaspoon ground black pepper
8 eggs	1 tablespoon cooking oil
3/4 cup grated Asiago or finely shredded Swiss cheese (3 ounces)	1/4 cup grated Asiago or finely shredded Swiss cheese (1 ounce)

1

Heat 1 tablespoon oil in a 10-inch broilerproof or regular skillet. Add onion and sweet pepper; cook for 2 to 3 minutes or until crisp-tender. Add mushrooms. Cook and stir for 3 minutes more.

2

Meanwhile, in a medium bowl use a fork to beat together the eggs, the 3/4 cup cheese, the basil, the water, salt, and black pepper until combined. Add 1 tablespoon oil to the skillet; heat. Pour egg mixture into skillet over vegetables. Cook over medium heat. As mixture sets, run a spatula around edge of skillet, lifting egg mixture so uncooked portion flows underneath. Continue cooking and lifting edge until mixture is almost set but still glossy and moist.

3

Sprinkle the 1/4 cup cheese on top. Place broilerproof skillet in broiler 4 to 5 inches from the heat; broil 1 to 2 minutes or just until top is set. (Or if using a regular skillet, remove skillet from heat; cover and let stand for 3 to 4 minutes or just until top is set.)

Nutrition Facts per serving: 365 calories, 25 g total fat, 445 mg cholesterol, 591 mg sodium, 9 g carbohydrate, 23 g protein.

RANCH EGGS

This fiery Mexican-style casserole is a flavor-packed way to start the day.
Or, serve it for a quick-and-easy supper.

Prep: 10 minutes **Bake:** 21 minutes **Makes:** 6 servings

1 large onion, halved lengthwise and
   thinly sliced
1 15-ounce can chunky chili-style
   tomato sauce
3 tablespoons snipped fresh cilantro
1 fresh jalapeño pepper,* seeded and
   chopped

6 eggs
¼ teaspoon salt
⅛ teaspoon ground black pepper
1 cup shredded Monterey Jack or
   cheddar cheese (4 ounces)
   Flour tortillas, warmed, or toast

1

Grease a 2-quart rectangular baking dish. Separate the onion into half-rings and place in prepared baking dish.

2

In a small bowl stir together the tomato sauce, cilantro, and jalapeño pepper. Pour the tomato mixture over onion. Break one of the eggs into a measuring cup. Carefully slide egg into tomato mixture. Repeat with the remaining eggs. Sprinkle the eggs with salt and black pepper.

3

Bake, uncovered, in a 400°F oven for 20 to 25 minutes or until the egg whites are completely set and yolks begin to thicken but are not hard. Sprinkle with cheese. Bake, uncovered, for 1 minute more. Serve with tortillas or toast.

Nutrition Facts per serving: 270 calories, 13 g total fat, 230 mg cholesterol, 736 mg sodium, 26 g carbohydrate, 15 g protein.

*Note: Because chile peppers, such as jalapeños, contain volatile oils that can burn your skin and eyes, avoid direct contract with them as much as possible. When working with chile peppers, wear plastic or rubber gloves. If your bare hands do touch the chile peppers, wash your hands and nails well with soap and warm water.

CHEESY EGG WEDGES

This versatile pie makes an enticing supper or brunch dish. Or for a party appetizer, slice it into 16 wedges.

Prep: 10 minutes **Bake:** 25 minutes **Makes:** 6 servings

4 beaten eggs
1/3 cup milk
1/4 cup all-purpose flour
1/2 teaspoon baking powder
1/8 teaspoon garlic powder
2 cups shredded cheddar or mozzarella cheese (8 ounces)

1 cup cream-style cottage cheese with chives
1 cup bottled meatless spaghetti sauce or salsa
Fresh basil sprigs (optional)

1

In a medium bowl use a rotary beater or wire whisk to beat together the eggs, milk, flour, baking powder, and garlic powder until combined. Stir in cheddar or mozzarella cheese and cottage cheese.

2

Lightly grease a 9-inch pie plate. Pour egg mixture into pie plate. Bake, uncovered, in a 375°F oven for 25 to 30 minutes or until golden brown and a knife inserted near the center comes out clean.

3

Meanwhile, in a small saucepan heat the spaghetti sauce or salsa over medium-low heat about 5 minutes or until warm, stirring occasionally.

4

To serve, cut egg mixture into wedges. Top with spaghetti sauce or salsa. If desired, garnish with basil.

Nutrition Facts per serving: 273 calories, 18 g total fat, 186 mg cholesterol, 614 mg sodium, 9 g carbohydrate, 20 g protein.

OLIVE-POTATO FRITTATA

Serve a tossed green salad with this cheese-topped egg-and-potato number,
and you've got the makings of the perfect light dinner.

Start to Finish: 30 minutes **Makes:** 4 servings

8 eggs
2 tablespoons snipped fresh oregano
    or 1 teaspoon dried oregano,
    crushed
1/4 teaspoon salt
2 tablespoons olive oil or cooking oil
2 medium potatoes (such as long
    white, round white, round red, or
    yellow), thinly sliced (2 cups)

1 medium onion, cut into thin wedges
1 teaspoon bottled minced garlic or
    2 cloves garlic, minced
1/4 teaspoon salt
1/4 teaspoon ground black pepper
1/2 cup sliced pitted ripe olives
1/4 cup finely shredded provolone or
    Parmesan cheese (1 ounce)

1
In a medium bowl use a fork to beat together the eggs, oregano, and 1/4 teaspoon salt. Set aside.

2
In a 10-inch broiler-proof or regular skillet heat oil. Add potatoes, onion, garlic, 1/4 teaspoon salt, and the black pepper. Cover and cook over medium heat for 5 minutes. Turn potato mixture with a spatula. Cover and cook for 5 to 6 minutes more or until potatoes are tender, turning mixture once more.

3
Pour egg mixture into skillet over the potato mixture. Sprinkle with olives. Cook over medium heat. As egg mixture sets, run a spatula around the edge of the skillet, lifting egg mixture to allow the uncooked portion to flow underneath. Continue cooking and lifting edge until egg mixture is almost set but still glossy and moist.

4
Place the broiler-proof skillet under broiler 4 to 5 inches from the heat; broil for 1 to 2 minutes or just until top is set. (Or, if using a regular skillet, remove the skillet from the heat; cover and let stand for 3 to 4 minutes or just until the top is set.) Sprinkle with cheese. Cut into 4 wedges.

Nutrition Facts per serving: 340 calories, 21 g total fat, 431 mg cholesterol, 671 mg sodium, 21 g carbohydrate, 17 g protein.

SPINACH-FETA FRITTATA

*All you need to round out this meal in a skillet is some crusty bread
and steamed or glazed baby carrots.*

Start to Finish: 25 minutes **Makes:** 4 servings

6 slightly beaten eggs
¼ cup milk
1 teaspoon dried dill
¼ teaspoon salt
¼ teaspoon ground black pepper
1 medium onion, chopped
½ teaspoon bottled minced garlic or
    1 clove garlic, minced

1 tablespoon margarine or butter
½ of a 10-ounce package frozen
    chopped spinach, thawed and well
    drained
¼ teaspoon lemon-pepper seasoning
¼ cup crumbled feta cheese (1 ounce)
    Chopped red sweet pepper
    (optional)

1

In a medium bowl use a fork to beat together the eggs, milk, dill, salt, and black pepper until
combined. Set aside.

2

In a 10-inch broilerproof or regular skillet cook onion and garlic in hot margarine or butter until
tender. Stir in spinach and lemon-pepper seasoning.

3

Pour egg mixture into the skillet over the spinach mixture. Cook over medium heat. As egg mixture
sets, run a spatula around the edge of the skillet, lifting egg mixture to allow the uncooked portion
to flow underneath. Continue cooking and lifting edge until egg mixture is almost set but still
glossy and moist.

4

Sprinkle with feta cheese. Place broilerproof skillet under the broiler 4 to 5 inches from the heat; broil
for 1 to 2 minutes or just until top is set. (Or if using a regular skillet, remove skillet from heat; cover
and let stand for 3 to 4 minutes or just until top is set.)

5

To serve, if desired, sprinkle with red sweet pepper. Cut into 8 wedges.

Nutrition Facts per serving: 206 calories, 14 g total fat, 335 mg cholesterol, 536 mg sodium, 6 g carbohydrate, 13 g protein.

VEGETABLE FRITTATA

When you're in the mood for a light meal, match this cheesy Italian-style omelet with a tossed salad and some breadsticks.

Start to Finish: 25 minutes **Makes:** 8 servings

1 cup water
1 cup broccoli florets
1/2 cup finely chopped carrot
1/4 cup sliced green onions
2 8-ounce cartons refrigerated or
    frozen egg product, thawed
1 tablespoon snipped fresh basil or
    1 teaspoon dried basil, crushed

1 tablespoon Dijon-style mustard
1/4 teaspoon ground black pepper
Nonstick cooking spray
3/4 cup shredded reduced-fat cheddar or
    Swiss cheese (3 ounces)
Tomato slices (optional)
Fresh tarragon sprigs (optional)

1

In a medium saucepan combine the water, broccoli, carrot, and green onions. Bring to boiling; reduce heat. Cover and simmer for 6 to 8 minutes or until vegetables are crisp-tender. Drain well.

2

In a medium bowl use a fork to beat together the egg product, basil, mustard, and pepper until combined. Coat an unheated large nonstick skillet with nonstick cooking spray. Preheat over medium heat. Spread the cooked vegetables in the bottom of the skillet. Sprinkle with half of the cheese. Pour egg product mixture over vegetables and cheese in skillet. As mixture sets, run a spatula around edge of skillet, lifting egg mixture so the uncooked portion flows underneath. Continue cooking and lifting the edge until egg mixture is almost set, but still glossy and moist. Remove from heat. Cover and let stand for 3 to 4 minutes or just until top is set.

3

To serve, cut the frittata into wedges. Sprinkle with the remaining cheese. If desired, garnish with tomato slices and tarragon sprigs.

Nutrition Facts per serving: 101 calories, 3 g total fat, 6 mg cholesterol, 287 mg sodium, 6 g carbohydrate, 11 g protein.

HUEVOS RANCHEROS

Add some warmed refried beans and flour tortillas, and you have a south-of-the-border meal that's terrific any time of day.

Start to Finish: 25 minutes **Makes:** 3 servings

1/2 cup chopped onion
1 tablespoon cooking oil
1 14¹/₂-ounce can tomatoes, cut up
2 tablespoons canned diced green chile peppers, drained and rinsed
1 teaspoon chili powder
1/8 teaspoon garlic powder
3 6-inch corn tortillas

1 teaspoon cooking oil
6 eggs
3/4 cup shredded Monterey Jack cheese or American cheese (3 ounces)
Fresh herb sprigs (optional)
Fresh chile peppers (optional)
Bottled hot pepper sauce
Lime wedges (optional)

1
In a large skillet cook onion in the 1 tablespoon oil until tender. Stir in undrained tomatoes, green chile peppers, chili powder, and garlic powder. Bring to boiling; reduce heat. Simmer, uncovered, for 5 to 10 minutes or until slightly thickened.

2
Meanwhile, place tortillas on a baking sheet; brush lightly with the 1 teaspoon oil. Bake in a 350°F oven about 10 minutes or until crisp.

3
Break one of the eggs into a measuring cup. Carefully slide egg into simmering tomato mixture. Repeat with remaining eggs. Cover and simmer gently for 3 to 5 minutes or until the whites are completely set and yolks begin to thicken but are not hard.

4
To serve, place each tortilla on a plate. Top each tortilla with 2 eggs. Spoon tomato mixture over eggs. Sprinkle with cheese. If desired, garnish with fresh herb sprigs and chile peppers. Serve with hot pepper sauce and, if desired, lime wedges.

Nutrition Facts per serving: 417 calories, 26 g total fat, 450 mg cholesterol, 514 mg sodium, 25 g carbohydrate, 23 g protein.

CREAMY POACHED EGGS

The rich double-cheese sauce turns simple poached eggs into an elegant brunch dish.

Start to Finish: 20 minutes **Makes:** 4 servings

$3/4$ cup shredded American cheese
(3 ounces)

1 3-ounce package cream cheese with chives, cut up

$1/2$ cup milk

$1/8$ teaspoon ground black pepper

4 eggs

2 English muffins or bagels, split and toasted

1

In a medium skillet combine American cheese, cream cheese, milk, and black pepper. Cook and stir over medium heat until the cheeses melt. Remove from heat.

2

Break one of the eggs into a measuring cup. Carefully slide egg into cheese mixture. Repeat with remaining eggs. Cover and cook over medium-low heat for 3 to 5 minutes or until the whites are completely set and yolks begin to thicken but are not hard.

3

Top each English muffin or bagel half with a cooked egg. Stir the cheese mixture with a wire whisk; spoon over eggs.

Nutrition Facts per serving: 312 calories, 20 g total fat, 259 mg cholesterol, 579 mg sodium, 16 g carbohydrate, 16 g protein.

CURRIED EGGS WITH LENTILS AND RICE

This no-fuss egg, lentil, and rice dish is a modern-day cousin of an
East Indian classic—kedgeree.

Start to Finish: 35 minutes **Makes:** 4 or 5 servings

1 cup chopped onion	3 beaten eggs
2 teaspoons curry powder	$\frac{1}{4}$ cup dairy sour cream
2 tablespoons olive oil	$\frac{1}{2}$ teaspoon salt
1 cup uncooked basmati rice	$\frac{1}{4}$ teaspoon ground nutmeg
3 cups vegetable broth or water	$\frac{1}{4}$ teaspoon ground black pepper
$\frac{1}{2}$ cup dry lentils	$\frac{1}{4}$ cup snipped fresh cilantro or parsley
1 tablespoon olive oil	

1

In a large saucepan cook and stir onion and curry powder in the 2 tablespoons oil over medium heat for 3 to 5 minutes or until onion is almost tender. Add rice; cook and stir for 3 minutes. Add broth or water and lentils. Bring to boiling; reduce heat. Cover and simmer for 20 to 25 minutes or just until lentils are tender and liquid is absorbed. (Do not overcook.)

2

Meanwhile, pour the 1 tablespoon oil into a wok or large skillet. Heat wok over medium heat. Pour the eggs into hot wok; lift and tilt the wok until eggs form a thin sheet. Cook, without stirring, about 2 minutes or just until eggs are set. Slide egg sheet out onto a cutting board. Cut into $\frac{3}{4}$-inch strips; set aside.

3

In a small bowl combine sour cream, salt, nutmeg, and black pepper. Stir into the rice mixture. Stir in the egg strips just until combined. Sprinkle each serving with cilantro or parsley.

Nutrition Facts per serving: 456 calories, 18 g total fat, 165 mg cholesterol, 1062 mg sodium, 58 g carbohydrate, 17 g protein.

PASTA

There's no end to the meatless meals you can create with pasta. Try one of these fantastic ideas to get started.

Rotini with Vegetable-Blue Cheese Sauce
(see recipe, page 70)

ASIAN VEGETABLE LO MEIN

Strips of cooked egg add color and protein to this healthful version of an Asian classic.

Start to Finish: 35 minutes **Makes:** 4 servings

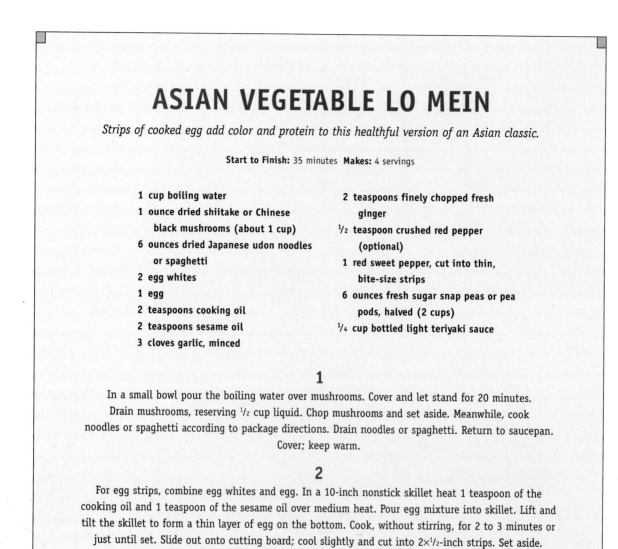

- 1 cup boiling water
- 1 ounce dried shiitake or Chinese black mushrooms (about 1 cup)
- 6 ounces dried Japanese udon noodles or spaghetti
- 2 egg whites
- 1 egg
- 2 teaspoons cooking oil
- 2 teaspoons sesame oil
- 3 cloves garlic, minced

- 2 teaspoons finely chopped fresh ginger
- 1/2 teaspoon crushed red pepper (optional)
- 1 red sweet pepper, cut into thin, bite-size strips
- 6 ounces fresh sugar snap peas or pea pods, halved (2 cups)
- 1/4 cup bottled light teriyaki sauce

1

In a small bowl pour the boiling water over mushrooms. Cover and let stand for 20 minutes. Drain mushrooms, reserving 1/2 cup liquid. Chop mushrooms and set aside. Meanwhile, cook noodles or spaghetti according to package directions. Drain noodles or spaghetti. Return to saucepan. Cover; keep warm.

2

For egg strips, combine egg whites and egg. In a 10-inch nonstick skillet heat 1 teaspoon of the cooking oil and 1 teaspoon of the sesame oil over medium heat. Pour egg mixture into skillet. Lift and tilt the skillet to form a thin layer of egg on the bottom. Cook, without stirring, for 2 to 3 minutes or just until set. Slide out onto cutting board; cool slightly and cut into 2×1/2-inch strips. Set aside.

3

Heat remaining cooking oil and remaining sesame oil in the same skillet over medium-high heat. Add mushrooms, garlic, ginger, and, if desired, crushed red pepper. Cook and stir for 1 minute. Add sweet pepper and sugar snap peas; cook and stir for 2 minutes more. Add reserved mushroom soaking liquid and teriyaki sauce. Bring to boiling; boil gently, uncovered, for 3 minutes. Add egg strips and vegetable mixture to noodles; toss well. Serve immediately.

Nutrition Facts per serving: 293 calories, 8 g total fat, 94 mg cholesterol, 307 mg sodium, 44 g carbohydrate, 12 g protein.

CAMPANELLE WITH ASIAGO SAUCE

If you can't find flower-shaped campanelle pasta, penne is a great alternative.

Start to Finish: 30 minutes **Makes:** 4 servings

8 ounces dried campanelle (bell flower pasta) or penne (mostaccioli)

2 small zucchini and/or yellow summer squash, halved lengthwise and sliced

½ cup snipped dried tomatoes (not oil packed), cut into strips

¼ cup dry white wine

¼ cup vegetable broth

2 cloves garlic, minced

2 tablespoons half-and-half or light cream

¾ cup grated Asiago or finely shredded Swiss cheese (3 ounces)

¼ cup coarsely chopped hazelnuts, toasted

2 tablespoons snipped fresh flat-leaf parsley

¼ teaspoon coarsely ground black pepper

1

In a Dutch oven cook pasta according to package directions, adding zucchini or yellow summer squash for the last 3 minutes of cooking. Drain pasta. Return to pan. Cover; keep warm.

2

Meanwhile, in a small saucepan combine the tomatoes, wine, broth, and garlic. Bring to boiling; reduce heat. Simmer, uncovered, about 3 minutes or until tomatoes are softened. Stir in half-and-half or light cream; heat through.

3

To serve, add tomato mixture, cheese, hazelnuts, 1 tablespoon of the parsley, and the pepper to pasta mixture. Toss to coat. Sprinkle with remaining parsley.

Nutrition Facts per serving: 410 calories, 16 g total fat, 25 mg cholesterol, 441 mg sodium, 51 g carbohydrate, 16 g protein.

CAVATELLI WITH ARUGULA AND DRIED CRANBERRIES

The sweetness of the dried cranberries counterbalances the peppery arugula in this toss-together pasta.

Start to Finish: 20 minutes **Makes:** 4 servings

8 ounces dried cavatelli or corkscrew macaroni (rotini)
$\frac{1}{2}$ cup vegetable broth
2 cloves garlic, minced
1 tablespoon olive oil
4 cups torn arugula and/or fresh spinach

$\frac{1}{2}$ cup dried cranberries or raisins
$\frac{1}{2}$ cup sliced almonds or coarsely chopped pistachio nuts, toasted
$\frac{1}{4}$ cup finely shredded Parmesan cheese (1 ounce)
Salt or sea salt (optional)

1

Cook pasta according to package directions. Drain pasta. Return to pan. Toss with broth. Cover; keep warm.

2

Meanwhile, in a large skillet cook garlic in hot oil over medium heat for 1 minute. Add arugula and/or spinach; cook and stir for 1 to 2 minutes or just until wilted.

3

To serve, in a large bowl combine pasta mixture, arugula mixture, cranberries, and nuts. Toss gently to combine. Sprinkle with Parmesan cheese. If desired, season to taste with salt.

Nutrition Facts per serving: 395 calories, 13 g total fat, 5 mg cholesterol, 331 mg sodium, 59 g carbohydrate, 14 g protein.

CHEESE TORTELLINI WITH, CANNELLINI BEAN SAUCE

Pureed cannellini beans make a smooth base for the creamy Parmesan cheese sauce.

Start to Finish: 20 minutes **Makes:** 4 servings

1 9-ounce package refrigerated cheese-filled tortellini

1 15-ounce can white kidney beans (cannellini beans), rinsed and drained

$^2/_3$ cup milk

$^2/_3$ cup red, yellow, and/or green sweet pepper cut into thin slivers

$^1/_4$ cup grated Parmesan cheese (1 ounce)

1 tablespoon snipped fresh oregano or 1 teaspoon dried oregano, crushed

$^1/_4$ teaspoon salt

$^1/_4$ teaspoon ground nutmeg

$^1/_4$ teaspoon ground black pepper

Finely shredded Parmesan cheese (optional)

Fresh oregano sprigs (optional)

Edible flowers (optional)

1

Cook the tortellini according to package directions. Drain tortellini. Return to pan. Cover; keep warm.

2

Meanwhile, for sauce, in a food processor bowl or blender container combine the white kidney beans and milk. Cover and process or blend until smooth. Transfer the bean mixture to a large skillet. Stir in sweet pepper, grated Parmesan cheese, snipped or dried oregano, salt, nutmeg, and black pepper. Cook and stir until mixture is heated through.

3

To serve, arrange pasta on dinner plates or a large platter. Spoon the sauce over pasta. If desired, sprinkle each serving with finely shredded Parmesan cheese. If desired, garnish with oregano sprigs and edible flowers.

Nutrition Facts per serving: 304 calories, 6 g total fat, 43 mg cholesterol, 730 mg sodium, 48 g carbohydrate, 21 g protein.

CHILI-SAUCED PASTA

Team this south-of-the-border pasta with a tossed spinach salad and corn bread.

Start to Finish: 20 minutes **Makes:** 3 servings

6 ounces refrigerated linguine or
   fettuccine
1 14^1/$_2$-ounce can low-sodium stewed
   tomatoes
1 medium green sweet pepper, cut
   into thin bite-size strips
2 tablespoons low-sodium tomato
   paste

1 tablespoon chili powder
^{1}/$_4$ teaspoon salt
^{1}/$_4$ teaspoon garlic powder
^{1}/$_4$ teaspoon ground cumin
1 8-ounce can red kidney beans,
   rinsed and drained
^{1}/$_4$ cup cold water
2 teaspoons cornstarch

1

Cook linguine according to package directions, except omit any salt. Drain linguine. Return to pan.
Cover; keep warm.

2

Meanwhile, in a medium saucepan combine tomatoes, sweet pepper, tomato paste, chili powder, salt, garlic
powder, and cumin. Bring to boiling; reduce heat. Cover and simmer for 3 minutes. Stir in kidney beans.

3

In a small bowl stir together the cold water and cornstarch; add to tomato mixture. Cook and stir until
thickened and bubbly. Cook and stir for 2 minutes more.

4

To serve, spoon tomato mixture over pasta.

Nutrition Facts per serving: 322 calories, 2 g total fat, 49 mg cholesterol, 392 mg sodium, 65 g carbohydrate, 15 g protein.

FETTUCCINE WITH GRILLED VEGETABLES

If you like, cook 4 ounces each spinach and plain fettuccine and mix them.

Start to Finish: 30 minutes **Makes:** 4 servings

1 small eggplant, peeled and cut into
   1-inch pieces
2 large fresh portobello mushrooms,
   stems removed and cut into
   1½-inch pieces
1 large green sweet pepper, cut into
   1-inch pieces
½ cup dry white wine
¼ cup water
1 vegetable bouillon cube
1 tablespoon cornstarch
1 tablespoon snipped fresh basil or
   1 teaspoon dried basil, crushed

2 teaspoons snipped fresh savory or
   ½ teaspoon dried savory, crushed
2 teaspoons snipped fresh thyme or
   ½ teaspoon dried thyme, crushed
8 ounces dried spinach fettuccine
   and/or plain fettuccine
1 small tomato, chopped (½ cup)
½ cup shredded reduced-fat mozzarella
   cheese (2 ounces)
2 tablespoons finely shredded
   Parmesan cheese
¼ teaspoon freshly ground black
   pepper

1

Alternately thread the eggplant cubes, mushroom pieces, and sweet pepper pieces onto metal skewers; set aside.

2

For sauce, in a saucepan combine wine, the water, bouillon cube, cornstarch, basil, savory, and thyme. Bring to boiling; reduce heat. Cook and stir until thickened and bubbly; cook and stir for 1 minute more. Keep warm.

3

Cook pasta according to package directions. Drain pasta. Return to pan. Cover; keep warm.

4

Meanwhile, brush kabobs with 1 to 2 tablespoons of the sauce. Grill kabobs on the rack of an uncovered grill directly over medium coals for 8 to 10 minutes or just until vegetables are tender, turning once halfway through grilling. (Or to broil kabobs, coat the unheated rack of a broiler pan with nonstick cooking spray. Place the kabobs on rack. Broil 3 to 4 inches from the heat for 8 to 10 minutes or just until vegetables are tender, turning once halfway through broiling.)

5

To serve, toss pasta with remaining sauce and arrange on 4 dinner plates. Slide the vegetables from skewers onto pasta. Sprinkle with tomato, mozzarella cheese, Parmesan cheese, and black pepper.

Nutrition Facts per serving: 354 calories, 5 g total fat, 10 mg cholesterol, 583 mg sodium, 58 g carbohydrate, 16 g protein.

ROTINI WITH ARUGULA, TOMATOES, AND OLIVES

If you prefer a less peppery flavor, substitute fresh spinach for the arugula.

Start to Finish: 30 minutes **Makes:** 4 servings

8 ounces dried corkscrew macaroni
   (rotini) or medium shell macaroni
3 cloves garlic, minced
¼ teaspoon crushed red pepper
2 tablespoons olive oil
3 to 4 cups torn arugula
¼ teaspoon salt

2 medium plum tomatoes, chopped
1 cup pitted niçoise or kalamata
   olives, halved
2 tablespoons snipped fresh parsley
¼ cup grated Parmesan cheese
   (1 ounce)

1

Cook pasta according to package directions. Drain pasta. Return to pan. Cover; keep warm.

2

Meanwhile, in a large skillet cook garlic and red pepper in hot olive oil for 3 to 4 minutes or until garlic is tender. Stir in arugula and salt. Cook and stir over medium heat just until arugula begins to wilt. Stir in tomatoes, olives, and parsley; heat through.

3

To serve, toss arugula mixture with pasta. Sprinkle with Parmesan cheese.

Nutrition Facts per serving: 379 calories, 14 g total fat, 5 mg cholesterol, 636 mg sodium, 51 g carbohydrate, 11 g protein.

LEMONY ALFREDO-STYLE FETTUCCINE

Pasta Alfredo doesn't have to be high in fat. Reduced-fat cream cheese and evaporated fat-free milk make this version rich and creamy, but with only 6 grams of fat per serving.

Start to Finish: 25 minutes **Makes:** 4 servings

2 cups loose-pack frozen broccoli, green beans, pearl onions, and red peppers or other frozen vegetable combination

8 ounces dried spinach fettuccine or plain fettuccine

2 ounces reduced-fat cream cheese (Neufchâtel), cut up

½ cup evaporated fat-free milk

¼ cup grated Parmesan cheese (1 ounce)

½ teaspoon finely shredded lemon peel

¼ teaspoon freshly ground black pepper

Dash ground nutmeg

1
Cook the mixed vegetables according to package directions, except omit any salt. Drain and keep warm.

2
Cook the fettuccine according to package directions, except omit any oil or salt. Drain fettuccine. Return to pan. Cover; keep warm.

3
Add cooked vegetables, cream cheese, evaporated milk, Parmesan cheese, lemon peel, pepper, and nutmeg to pasta in pan. Heat through, tossing gently until cream cheese is melted and fettuccine is well coated. Serve immediately.

Nutrition Facts per serving: 339 calories, 6 g total fat, 17 mg cholesterol, 256 mg sodium, 55 g carbohydrate, 16 g protein.

LO MEIN WITH TOFU

Japanese soba noodles are made from buckwheat flour and are sold in Asian specialty stores.

Start to Finish: 25 minutes **Makes:** 4 servings

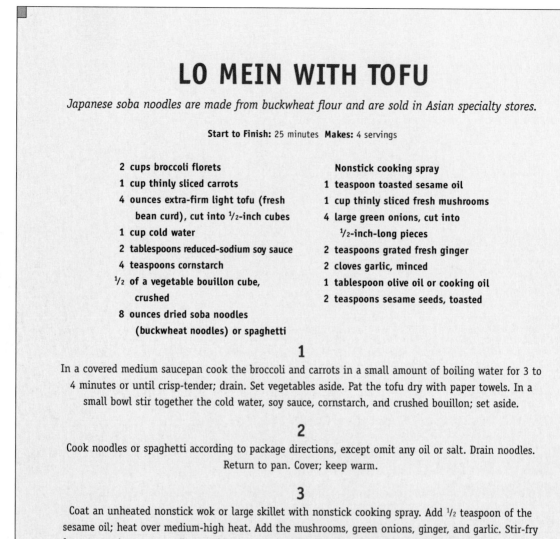

2 cups broccoli florets
1 cup thinly sliced carrots
4 ounces extra-firm light tofu (fresh
    bean curd), cut into ¹/₂-inch cubes
1 cup cold water
2 tablespoons reduced-sodium soy sauce
4 teaspoons cornstarch
¹/₂ of a vegetable bouillon cube,
    crushed
8 ounces dried soba noodles
    (buckwheat noodles) or spaghetti

Nonstick cooking spray
1 teaspoon toasted sesame oil
1 cup thinly sliced fresh mushrooms
4 large green onions, cut into
    ¹/₂-inch-long pieces
2 teaspoons grated fresh ginger
2 cloves garlic, minced
1 tablespoon olive oil or cooking oil
2 teaspoons sesame seeds, toasted

1

In a covered medium saucepan cook the broccoli and carrots in a small amount of boiling water for 3 to 4 minutes or until crisp-tender; drain. Set vegetables aside. Pat the tofu dry with paper towels. In a small bowl stir together the cold water, soy sauce, cornstarch, and crushed bouillon; set aside.

2

Cook noodles or spaghetti according to package directions, except omit any oil or salt. Drain noodles. Return to pan. Cover; keep warm.

3

Coat an unheated nonstick wok or large skillet with nonstick cooking spray. Add ¹/₂ teaspoon of the sesame oil; heat over medium-high heat. Add the mushrooms, green onions, ginger, and garlic. Stir-fry for 1 to 2 minutes or until vegetables are crisp-tender. Remove vegetables. Add the olive oil or cooking oil and remaining sesame oil to the wok. Add the tofu; stir-fry for 1 to 2 minutes or just until tofu starts to brown. Remove tofu. Add broccoli-carrot mixture and mushroom mixture to the wok; push vegetables from center of the wok. Stir the soy sauce mixture; add to center of wok. Cook and stir until thickened and bubbly.

4

Add the noodles to the wok or skillet. Using 2 spatulas or forks, lightly toss the mixture for 3 to 4 minutes or until noodles are heated through. Add the tofu; toss lightly. Cover; cook for 1 to 2 minutes or until heated through. To serve, sprinkle noodle mixture with sesame seeds.

Nutrition Facts per serving: 241 calories, 5 g total fat, 0 mg cholesterol, 704 mg sodium, 43 g carbohydrate, 10 g protein.

PASTA WITH GREEN BEANS AND GOAT CHEESE

Goat cheese adds a delectable tang to this vegetable, walnut, and pasta combo.

Start to Finish: 30 minutes **Makes:** 6 servings

8 ounces dried linguine

1 9-ounce package frozen cut green beans

2 tablespoons olive oil

1 tablespoon margarine or butter

2 medium leeks, thinly sliced (about ²/₃ cup)

¹/₂ cup chopped walnuts

1 tablespoon snipped fresh thyme or marjoram

4 ounces semisoft goat cheese (chèvre), crumbled

Cracked black pepper

1

In a 4-quart Dutch oven cook linguine according to package directions, adding green beans for the last 5 minutes of cooking. Drain. Set aside.

2

In the same Dutch oven heat oil and margarine or butter over medium heat. Cook leeks and walnuts in hot oil and margarine for 3 to 4 minutes or until leeks are tender and walnuts are lightly toasted. Stir in thyme or marjoram. Stir in drained linguine and green beans; heat through.

3

To serve, sprinkle pasta mixture with goat cheese and pepper.

Nutrition Facts per serving: 351 calories, 19 g total fat, 15 mg cholesterol, 125 mg sodium, 35 g carbohydrate, 11 g protein.

PASTA WITH PRIMAVERA SAUCE

Just about any pasta will work in this dish, but cavatelli and mostaccioli are nice because their ridges help capture the colorful vegetable-and-cheese sauce.

Start to Finish: 25 minutes **Makes:** 4 servings

- 8 ounces dried cavatelli and/or penne (mostaccioli)
- 3 cups loose-pack frozen broccoli, cauliflower, and carrots
- ³/₄ cup fat-free milk
- 2 tablespoons all-purpose flour
- ¹/₂ of a vegetable bouillon cube, crushed
- ³/₄ teaspoon fines herbes
- ¹/₄ teaspoon ground black pepper
- ³/₄ cup plain fat-free yogurt
- ³/₄ cup shredded reduced-fat Monterey Jack cheese (3 ounces)
- 2 tablespoons snipped fresh parsley
- 2 tablespoons grated Parmesan cheese

1
In a large saucepan cook pasta according to package directions, adding vegetables for the last 3 minutes of cooking time.

2
Meanwhile, for sauce, in a medium saucepan stir together the milk, flour, bouillon, fines herbes, and pepper. Cook and stir over medium heat until mixture is thickened and bubbly. Stir in yogurt, Monterey Jack cheese, and parsley; cook and stir until cheese is melted (do not boil).

3
To serve, drain pasta and vegetables. Toss with sauce to coat. Divide among 4 dinner plates. Sprinkle with Parmesan cheese.

Nutrition Facts per serving: 374 calories, 6 g total fat, 19 mg cholesterol, 498 mg sodium, 58 g carbohydrate, 21 g protein.

ROASTED RED PEPPER SAUCE OVER TORTELLINI

Thyme and oregano infuse the roasted pepper sauce with a subtle herb flavor that blends wonderfully with the cheese tortellini.

Start to Finish: 20 minutes **Makes:** 3 servings

1 9-ounce package refrigerated cheese-filled tortellini

1 12-ounce jar roasted red sweet peppers, drained

¹/₂ cup chopped onion

3 cloves garlic, minced

1 tablespoon margarine or butter

2 teaspoons snipped fresh thyme or ¹/₂ teaspoon dried thyme, crushed

2 teaspoons snipped fresh oregano or ¹/₄ teaspoon dried oregano, crushed

1 teaspoon sugar

Fresh thyme sprigs (optional)

1
Cook tortellini according to package directions. Drain tortellini. Return to pan. Cover; keep warm.

2
Meanwhile, place the roasted sweet peppers in a food processor bowl. Cover and process until smooth. Set aside.

3
For sauce, in a medium saucepan cook the onion and garlic in hot margarine or butter until onion is tender. Add pureed peppers, snipped or dried thyme, oregano, and sugar. Cook and stir until heated through. Pour sauce over pasta; toss gently to coat.

4
To serve, transfer to a warm serving dish. If desired, garnish with thyme sprigs.

Nutrition Facts per serving: 337 calories, 10 g total fat, 40 mg cholesterol, 358 mg sodium, 49 g carbohydrate, 14 g protein.

TERIYAKI PENNE

Ginger, garlic, and teriyaki sauce give this no-fuss pasta a triple flavor boost.

Start to Finish: 25 minutes **Makes:** 4 servings

- 8 ounces dried tomato-basil or plain penne (mostaccioli)
- 1 clove garlic, minced
- ½ teaspoon grated fresh ginger
- 1 tablespoon toasted sesame oil or cooking oil

- 3 cups packaged shredded broccoli (broccoli slaw mix)
- 2 cups sliced fresh mushrooms
- ¼ cup bottled teriyaki sauce
- ¼ cup thinly sliced green onions

1

Cook pasta according to package directions. Drain pasta. Return to saucepan. Cover; keep warm.

2

Meanwhile, in a large skillet cook garlic and ginger in hot oil for 15 seconds. Stir in the broccoli, mushrooms, and teriyaki sauce. Cook and stir about 5 minutes or until broccoli is crisp-tender.

3

To serve, toss broccoli mixture with hot pasta. Sprinkle with green onions.

Nutrition Facts per serving: 286 calories, 5 g total fat, 0 mg cholesterol, 749 mg sodium, 50 g carbohydrate, 11 g protein.

PENNE WITH RICOTTA AND SUMMER VEGETABLES

Juicy ripe tomatoes star in this one-dish meal.

Start to Finish: 30 minutes **Makes:** 4 servings

8 ounces dried penne (mostaccioli) or cut ziti
2½ cups broccoli florets
1½ cups cut fresh asparagus or green beans (1-inch pieces)
2 large tomatoes
1 cup light ricotta cheese
¼ cup snipped fresh basil
4 teaspoons snipped fresh thyme

4 teaspoons balsamic vinegar
1 tablespoon olive oil
1 clove garlic, minced
½ teaspoon salt
½ teaspoon freshly ground black pepper
2 tablespoons grated Parmesan or Romano cheese
Fresh basil sprigs (optional)

1

Cook pasta according to package directions, adding broccoli and asparagus or green beans for the last 3 minutes of cooking. Drain.

2

Meanwhile, place a fine strainer over a large bowl. Cut tomatoes in half; squeeze seeds and juice into strainer. With the back of a spoon, press seeds against strainer to extract juice; discard seeds. Chop tomatoes. Add ricotta cheese, snipped basil, thyme, balsamic vinegar, oil, garlic, salt, and pepper to tomato juice; mix well. Stir tomatoes into ricotta mixture.

3

Add hot pasta-vegetable mixture to ricotta mixture. Toss to coat all ingredients. Divide mixture among 4 dinner plates; sprinkle with Parmesan or Romano cheese. If desired, garnish with basil sprigs.

Nutrition Facts per serving: 368 calories, 8 g total fat, 12 mg cholesterol, 393 mg sodium, 57 g carbohydrate, 19 g protein.

HERBED PASTA PRIMAVERA

A stir-fried vegetable medley makes this pasta both colorful and tasty.

Start to Finish: 25 minutes   **Makes:** 4 servings

6 ounces dried linguine, spaghetti, or
    fettuccine
1 cup cold water
2 teaspoons cornstarch
1 vegetable bouillon cube, crushed
1 tablespoon olive oil
2 cloves garlic, minced
8 ounces fresh asparagus, cut into
    1-inch pieces

2 medium carrots, thinly bias-sliced
1 medium onion, chopped
1 6-ounce package frozen pea pods,
    thawed and well drained
$^2/_3$ cup sliced almonds
$^1/_4$ cup snipped fresh parsley
1$^1/_2$ teaspoons dried basil, crushed
$^1/_4$ teaspoon ground black pepper
$^1/_3$ cup finely shredded Parmesan cheese

1

Cook pasta according to package directions. Drain pasta. Return to pan. Cover; keep warm. Meanwhile, for sauce, in a small bowl stir together the water, cornstarch, and crushed bouillon. Set aside.

2

In a wok or large skillet heat oil over medium-high heat. Stir-fry garlic in hot oil for 15 seconds. Add asparagus, carrots, and onion; stir-fry for 2 minutes. Add pea pods, almonds, parsley, basil, and pepper. Stir-fry about 1 minute more or until vegetables are crisp-tender. Remove vegetable mixture from wok.

3

Stir sauce; add to wok. Cook and stir until thickened and bubbly. Cook and stir for 1 minute more. Return vegetable mixture to wok. Cook and stir until heated through.

4

To serve, spoon vegetable mixture over pasta. Sprinkle with Parmesan cheese.

Nutrition Facts per serving: 432 calories, 19 g total fat, 7 mg cholesterol, 642 mg sodium, 52 g carbohydrate, 17 g protein.

ROTINI WITH VEGETABLE-BLUE CHEESE SAUCE

A little blue cheese goes a long way in this pasta dish, giving it a rich, tangy flavor. (Pictured on page 39.)

Start to Finish: 25 minutes **Makes:** 3 or 4 servings

6 ounces dried corkscrew macaroni (rotini)

1 10-ounce package frozen cut asparagus

2 medium carrots, thinly sliced

1 12-ounce can (1¹/₂ cups) evaporated fat-free milk

2 tablespoons all-purpose flour

1¹/₂ teaspoons snipped fresh marjoram or ¹/₂ teaspoon dried marjoram, crushed

¹/₃ cup crumbled blue cheese

Fresh marjoram sprigs (optional)

1

Cook pasta according to package directions, except omit any oil or salt. Drain pasta. Return to pan. Cover; keep warm.

2

Meanwhile, cook the asparagus according to package directions, adding carrots for the last 5 minutes of cooking. Drain and keep warm.

3

In a medium saucepan stir the evaporated milk into the flour; add snipped or dried marjoram. Cook and stir over medium heat until thickened and bubbly. Cook and stir for 1 minute more. Stir in the asparagus and carrots. Heat through; remove from heat. Add the blue cheese; stir until cheese is melted.

4

To serve, spoon cheese mixture over pasta. If desired, garnish with marjoram sprigs.

Nutrition Facts per serving: 314 calories, 5 g total fat, 11 mg cholesterol, 281 mg sodium, 52 g carbohydrate, 17 g protein.

ORZO WITH ROOT VEGETABLES

Here's a newfangled twist on rice pilaf. This colorful combo is made with orzo instead of rice and is loaded with veggies and red beans.

Start to Finish: 30 minutes   **Makes:** 4 servings

1 large onion, halved and thinly sliced
2 cloves garlic, minced
1 tablespoon olive oil
1 14-ounce can vegetable broth or chicken broth
$1/4$ cup water
$1/2$ teaspoon dried thyme, crushed
$1/8$ teaspoon ground red pepper
$3/4$ cup orzo (rosamarina)

2 medium carrots, cut into thin bite-size strips
1 15-ounce can red beans, rinsed and drained
1 medium turnip, cut into thin bite-size strips
1 medium red sweet pepper, cut into thin bite-size strips

1

In a large saucepan cook onion and garlic in hot oil just until tender. Stir in broth, the water, thyme, and ground red pepper. Bring to boiling. Add orzo and carrots. Return to boiling; reduce heat. Cover and simmer for 10 minutes.

2

Stir red beans, turnip, and sweet pepper into mixture in saucepan. Return to boiling; reduce heat. Cover and simmer for 2 to 3 minutes more or until orzo is tender.

Nutrition Facts per serving: 243 calories, 5 g total fat, 0 mg cholesterol, 622 mg sodium, 44 g carbohydrate, 12 g protein.

CRIMSON PASTA TOSS

This pasta gets its name from the bits of dried tomato and chipotle pepper in the tofu sauce.

Start to Finish: 25 minutes **Makes:** 6 servings

12 ounces dried corkscrew macaroni (rotini), penne (mostaccioli), or cut ziti

1 12-ounce package firm light tofu (fresh bean curd), drained

¼ cup oil-packed dried tomatoes,* drained

¼ cup vegetable broth

1 teaspoon dried oregano,* crushed

1 teaspoon dried basil,* crushed

1 to 2 canned chipotle peppers in adobo sauce

2 cloves garlic, minced

½ teaspoon salt

Finely shredded fresh basil (optional)

Shaved Parmesan cheese (optional)

Cherry tomatoes, quartered (optional)

1

Cook pasta according to package directions. Drain pasta. Return to pan. Cover; keep warm.

2

Meanwhile, in a blender container or food processor bowl combine tofu, dried tomatoes, broth, dried oregano, dried basil, chipotle peppers, garlic, and salt. Cover and blend or process until nearly smooth.

3

To serve, toss tofu mixture with cooked pasta in the pan; heat through. If desired, garnish with finely shredded basil, Parmesan cheese, and cherry tomatoes.

Nutrition Facts per serving: 258 calories, 3 g total fat, 0 mg cholesterol, 297 mg sodium, 47 g carbohydrate, 11 g protein.

*Note: If desired, substitute 3 tablespoons purchased dried tomato pesto for the dried tomatoes, dried oregano, and dried basil.

TRATTORIA-STYLE SPINACH FETTUCCINE

This elegant entrée is just like those served in quaint Italian restaurants.

Start to Finish: 25 minutes **Makes:** 4 servings

1 9-ounce package refrigerated
   spinach fettuccine
2 tablespoons chopped shallot or
   green onion
1 medium carrot, coarsely shredded
   (about $1/2$ cup)
1 tablespoon olive oil

4 medium red and/or yellow tomatoes
   (about $1^1/4$ pounds), coarsely
   chopped ($2^2/3$ cups)
$1/4$ cup oil-packed dried tomatoes,
   drained and snipped
$1/2$ cup crumbled garlic and herb or
   peppercorn feta cheese (2 ounces)

1

Using kitchen scissors, cut fettuccine strands in half crosswise. Cook fettuccine according to package directions. Drain fettuccine. Return to pan. Cover; keep warm.

2

Meanwhile, in a large skillet cook shallot or green onion and carrot in hot oil over medium heat for 1 to 2 minutes or just until tender. Stir in fresh and dried tomatoes; cook for 1 to 2 minutes more or until heated through.

3

To serve, spoon tomato mixture over pasta; toss gently. Sprinkle each serving with cheese.

Nutrition Facts per serving: 311 calories, 11 g total fat, 72 mg cholesterol, 243 mg sodium, 44 g carbohydrate, 13 g protein.

MEXICAN-STYLE PASTA

For a change of pace, add $^1/_2$ cup frozen whole kernel corn to the vegetables with the tomatoes.

Start to Finish: 30 minutes **Makes:** 4 servings

1 cup dried wagon wheel macaroni
   (ruote) or elbow macaroni
1 cup chopped onion
$^1/_2$ cup chopped green sweet pepper
2 teaspoons olive oil or cooking oil
$1^1/_2$ to 2 teaspoons chili powder
1 $14^1/_2$-ounce can low-sodium
   tomatoes, cut up

1 8-ounce can tomato sauce
$^1/_2$ teaspoon garlic powder
$^1/_8$ teaspoon ground red pepper
1 $15^1/_2$-ounce can reduced-sodium red
   kidney beans, rinsed and drained
$^1/_4$ cup shredded reduced-fat cheddar
   cheese (1 ounce)

1

Cook pasta according to package directions, except omit any oil or salt. Drain pasta. Return to pan. Cover; keep warm.

2

Meanwhile, in a medium saucepan cook and stir onion and sweet pepper in hot oil over medium-high heat about 3 minutes or until vegetables are tender. Stir in the chili powder; cook and stir for 1 minute. Stir in the undrained tomatoes, tomato sauce, garlic powder, and ground red pepper. Bring to boiling; reduce heat. Simmer, uncovered, about 15 minutes or until desired consistency, stirring often.

3

Stir kidney beans and hot cooked pasta into tomato mixture; heat through.

4

To serve, sprinkle with cheddar cheese.

Nutrition Facts per serving: 261 calories, 5 g total fat, 5 mg cholesterol, 562 mg sodium, 47 g carbohydrate, 13 g protein.

NUTTY ORZO AND VEGETABLES

Orzo is a rice-shaped pasta that's sometimes labeled rosamarina. Look for it with the other pastas at your supermarket.

Start to Finish: 20 minutes **Makes:** 4 servings

½ cup dried orzo (rosamarina)
1 cup loose-pack frozen broccoli
    florets
1 cup zucchini cut into ¾-inch pieces
1 15-ounce can chickpeas (garbanzo
    beans), rinsed and drained
1 14½-ounce can low-sodium stewed
    tomatoes

1¼ cups bottled light spaghetti sauce
1 tablespoon snipped fresh thyme
¼ cup chopped dry roasted cashews or
    slivered almonds, toasted
¼ cup shredded reduced-fat mozzarella
    cheese (1 ounce)

1

Cook orzo according to package directions, except omit any salt; add broccoli and zucchini after 5 minutes of cooking. Drain orzo and vegetables; return to pan. Add chickpeas, undrained tomatoes, spaghetti sauce, and thyme. Bring to boiling; reduce heat. Cover and simmer for 5 minutes. Stir in cashews or almonds.

2

Sprinkle each serving with mozzarella cheese.

Nutrition Facts per serving: 382 calories, 10 g total fat, 3 mg cholesterol, 398 mg sodium, 58 g carbohydrate, 15 g protein.

PASTA AND SICILIAN TOMATO SAUCE

This no-cook sauce goes together in less time than it takes to cook the pasta.

Start to Finish: 20 minutes **Makes:** 4 servings

8 ounces dried penne (mostaccioli)
$\frac{1}{4}$ cup pine nuts or chopped almonds
$\frac{1}{4}$ cup grated Parmesan cheese
    (1 ounce)
1 teaspoon bottled minced garlic or
    2 cloves garlic, minced
2 cups loosely packed fresh basil
    leaves

$\frac{1}{4}$ cup olive oil
$1\frac{1}{2}$ pounds tomatoes, peeled, seeded,
    and cut into chunks
$\frac{1}{2}$ teaspoon salt
$\frac{1}{8}$ teaspoon ground black pepper
    Fresh basil (optional)

1

Cook pasta according to package directions. Drain pasta. Return to pan. Cover; keep warm.

2

Meanwhile, for sauce, in a food processor bowl combine the nuts, Parmesan cheese, and garlic. Cover and process until chopped. Add about half of the loosely packed basil and the oil. Cover and process until the basil is chopped, stopping the machine occasionally to scrape down the side. Add the remaining loosely packed basil; cover and process until the basil is chopped, stopping the machine occasionally to scrape down the side. Add the tomatoes and process with several on/off turns. (The tomatoes should remain chunky. If the mixture is too smooth, add some chopped fresh tomato.) Stir in the salt and pepper.

3

To serve, spoon sauce over pasta. If desired, garnish with additional fresh basil.

Nutrition Facts per serving: 459 calories, 22 g total fat, 5 mg cholesterol, 400 mg sodium, 55 g carbohydrate, 14 g protein.

PASTA ROSA-VERDE

For a vegetarian meal that's fresh and quick, stir together garlic-seasoned tomatoes and greens to top off hot cooked pasta.

Start to Finish: 30 minutes **Makes:** 4 servings

8 ounces dried ziti or mostaccioli

1 medium onion, thinly sliced

2 cloves garlic, minced

1 tablespoon olive oil

4 to 6 medium tomatoes, seeded and coarsely chopped (3 cups)

1 teaspoon salt

$1/2$ teaspoon freshly ground black pepper

$1/4$ teaspoon crushed red pepper (optional)

3 cups coarsely chopped arugula, watercress, and/or fresh spinach

$1/4$ cup pine nuts or slivered almonds, toasted

2 tablespoons crumbled Gorgonzola or other blue cheese

1

Cook pasta according to package directions. Drain pasta. Return to saucepan. Cover and keep warm.

2

Meanwhile, in a large skillet cook onion and garlic in hot oil over medium heat until onion is tender. Add tomatoes, salt, black pepper, and, if desired, crushed red pepper. Cook and stir over medium-high heat about 2 minutes or until the tomatoes are warm and release some of their juices. Stir in arugula, watercress, or spinach and heat just until greens wilt.

3

To serve, divide pasta among 4 dinner plates. Top with tomato mixture. Sprinkle with nuts and cheese.

Nutrition Facts per serving: 352 calories, 11 g total fat, 3 mg cholesterol, 610 mg sodium, 54 g carbohydrate, 12 g protein.

TORTELLINI, GREEN AND SIMPLE

Refrigerated tortellini make this meatless meal fast and delicious!

Start to Finish: 20 minutes **Makes:** 3 servings

1 9-ounce package refrigerated
  cheese-filled tortellini
½ cup frozen peas
1 cup broccoli florets

¼ cup shredded fontina or Swiss
  cheese (1 ounce)
1 tablespoon olive oil
2 teaspoons snipped fresh oregano
¼ teaspoon crushed red pepper

1

Cook pasta according to package directions, adding peas and broccoli to the water with pasta. Drain.
Return pasta and vegetables to saucepan.

2

Add cheese, oil, oregano, and crushed red pepper to pasta mixture; toss to coat.

Nutrition Facts per serving: 364 calories, 14 g total fat, 51 mg cholesterol, 421 mg sodium, 44 g carbohydrate, 18 g protein.

PASTA WITH THREE CHEESES

Take your choice of Gouda, Edam, Havarti, fontina, cheddar, or Swiss cheese to team with the cream cheese and Parmesan cheese. Each option gives you different but equally yummy results.

Start to Finish: 30 minutes **Makes:** 4 servings

10 ounces dried medium shell macaroni
or corkscrew macaroni (rotini)

2 cups loose-pack frozen cauliflower,
broccoli, and carrots or other
vegetable combination

1 cup milk

1 3-ounce package cream cheese,
cut up

¼ teaspoon coarsely ground black
pepper

¾ cup shredded Gouda, Edam, Havarti,
fontina, cheddar, or Swiss cheese
(3 ounces)

¼ cup grated Parmesan cheese
(1 ounce)

Grated Parmesan cheese (optional)

1
In a large saucepan cook pasta according to package directions, adding the frozen vegetables for the last 5 minutes of cooking. Drain.

2
In the hot saucepan combine milk, cream cheese, and pepper. Cook and stir over low heat until cream cheese is melted.

3
Return pasta mixture to saucepan. Toss to coat with cream cheese mixture. Gently stir in the shredded cheese and the ¼ cup Parmesan cheese.

4
To serve, transfer to a serving bowl. If desired, sprinkle with additional Parmesan cheese.

Nutrition Facts per serving: 598 calories, 25 g total fat, 86 mg cholesterol, 596 mg sodium, 66 g carbohydrate, 28 g protein.

SPAGHETTI WITH VEGETARIAN SAUCE BOLOGNESE

You'll be amazed at how the cereal gives the sauce a meatlike texture.

Start to Finish: 25 minutes **Makes:** 4 servings

- 8 ounces dried spaghetti
- ½ cup finely chopped carrot
- ½ cup thinly sliced celery
- 1 medium onion, finely chopped
- ½ teaspoon dried oregano, crushed
- ¼ teaspoon ground black pepper
- 1 tablespoon olive oil
- 1½ teaspoons bottled minced garlic or 3 cloves garlic, minced
- ¾ cup Grape-Nuts cereal
- 1 14½-ounce can Italian-style stewed tomatoes
- 1 8-ounce can tomato sauce
- ¼ to ½ cup water
- 1 tablespoon olive oil
- Grated Parmesan or Romano cheese (optional)
- Fresh oregano sprigs (optional)

1

Cook spaghetti according to package directions. Meanwhile, in a medium saucepan cook carrot, celery, onion, dried oregano, and pepper in 1 tablespoon hot olive oil over medium-high heat until onion is tender. Add garlic; cook for 1 minute more. Stir in the cereal. Add the undrained tomatoes, tomato sauce, and desired amount of the water. Bring to boiling; reduce heat. Cover and simmer for 5 to 10 minutes or until desired consistency.

2

To serve, drain spaghetti. Toss with 1 tablespoon olive oil. Divide the spaghetti among 4 dinner plates. Spoon sauce over pasta. If desired, sprinkle with Parmesan or Romano cheese and garnish with oregano sprigs.

Nutrition Facts per serving: 416 calories, 8 g total fat, 0 mg cholesterol, 907 mg sodium, 76 g carbohydrate, 12 g protein.

ANGEL HAIR WITH ASPARAGUS, TOMATOES, AND FRESH BASIL

Take a trip to your local farmer's market to pick up the asparagus, tomatoes, and basil for this cream-of-the-crop entrée.

Start to Finish: 20 minutes **Makes:** 3 servings

1 9-ounce package refrigerated angel hair (capellini)
1 pound fresh asparagus spears
4 cloves garlic, thinly sliced
$\frac{1}{4}$ teaspoon ground black pepper
1 tablespoon olive oil

6 medium plum tomatoes, seeded and chopped ($2\frac{1}{4}$ cups)
$\frac{1}{4}$ cup dry white wine
$\frac{1}{4}$ teaspoon salt
1 tablespoon butter or margarine
$\frac{1}{4}$ cup shredded fresh basil

1
Cook pasta according to package directions. Drain pasta. Return to pan. Cover; keep warm.

2
Meanwhile, snap off and discard woody bases from asparagus. Remove the tips; set aside. Bias-slice the remaining portions of asparagus spears into 1- to $1\frac{1}{2}$-inch-long pieces; set aside.

3
In a large skillet cook and stir garlic and pepper in hot oil over medium heat for 1 minute. Add the tomatoes; cook for 2 minutes more, stirring often. Add the asparagus pieces, wine, and salt to the skillet. Cook, uncovered, for 3 minutes. Add the asparagus tips. Cook, uncovered, for 1 minute more. Add butter and stir until melted.

4
To serve, add asparagus mixture and basil to pasta; toss to coat.

Nutrition Facts per serving: 484 calories, 11 g total fat, 10 mg cholesterol, 238 mg sodium, 81 g carbohydrate, 15 g protein.

GRAINS, BEANS & VEGETABLES

When you face the dilemma of what to cook for dinner, let one of these family pleasers come to the rescue.

Southwestern Black Bean Cakes with
Guacamole (see recipe, page 99)

SPICY BLACK BEANS AND RICE

If you have a little extra time, squares of fresh-from-the-oven corn bread are a scrumptious alternative to the rice.

Start to Finish: 30 minutes **Makes:** 4 servings

1 medium onion, chopped
4 cloves garlic, minced
2 tablespoons olive oil or cooking oil
1 15-ounce can black beans, rinsed and drained
1 14^1/$_2$-ounce can Mexican-style stewed tomatoes

^{1}/$_8$ to ^{1}/$_4$ teaspoon ground red pepper
2 cups hot cooked brown or long grain rice
Chopped onion (optional)

1

In a medium saucepan cook the medium onion and the garlic in hot oil until onion is tender. Carefully stir in beans, undrained tomatoes, and ground red pepper. Bring to boiling; reduce heat. Simmer, uncovered, for 15 minutes.

2

To serve, mound rice on 4 dinner plates; make a well in the center of each. Spoon black bean mixture into centers. If desired, sprinkle with additional chopped onion.

Nutrition Facts per serving: 279 calories, 8 g total fat, 0 mg cholesterol, 631 mg sodium, 47 g carbohydrate, 11 g protein.

BEANS WITH SPAGHETTI SQUASH

Tender, golden strands of squash are just the thing to sop up juices from the zesty bean and roasted pepper mixture.

Start to Finish: 30 minutes   **Makes:** 4 servings

1 2$\frac{1}{2}$- to 3-pound spaghetti squash, halved and seeded

1 10-ounce package frozen baby lima beans

1 15-ounce can red kidney beans, rinsed and drained

$\frac{1}{2}$ of a 7-ounce jar roasted red sweet peppers, rinsed, drained, and cut into bite-size strips

$\frac{1}{2}$ teaspoon salt

$\frac{1}{4}$ cup balsamic vinegar

3 tablespoons olive oil

1 tablespoon honey mustard

2 cloves garlic, minced

Freshly ground black pepper (optional)

1

Place squash halves in a large Dutch oven with about 1 inch of water. Bring to boiling; reduce heat. Cover and cook for 15 to 20 minutes or until squash is tender.

2

Meanwhile, in a large saucepan cook lima beans according to package directions, adding kidney beans for the last 3 minutes of cooking. Drain; return beans to saucepan. Stir in roasted red peppers and salt; heat through.

3

For dressing, in a screw-top jar combine the balsamic vinegar, oil, honey mustard, and garlic. Cover and shake well. Pour over warm bean mixture; toss gently to coat.

4

Drain squash. Using a fork, scrape the squash pulp from the shells in strands; return strands to each shell. Spoon the warm bean mixture over squash strands in shells; drizzle with any extra dressing.

5

To serve, cut each squash shell in half. If desired, sprinkle with black pepper.

Nutrition Facts per serving: 421 calories, 11 g total fat, 0 mg cholesterol, 466 mg sodium, 65 g carbohydrate, 21 g protein.

ITALIAN THREE-BEAN AND RICE SKILLET

The whole meal is in this Italian-seasoned skillet. Just add some dinner rolls or biscuits and finish off the meal with fruit or ice cream.

Start to Finish: 30 minutes **Makes:** 4 servings

1 15- to 15½-ounce can small red beans or red kidney beans, rinsed and drained

1 14½-ounce can Italian-style stewed tomatoes

1 cup vegetable broth

¾ cup quick-cooking brown rice

½ of a 10-ounce package frozen baby lima beans

½ of a 9-ounce package frozen cut green beans

½ teaspoon dried basil, crushed, or dried Italian seasoning, crushed

1 cup bottled meatless spaghetti sauce

2 ounces thinly sliced mozzarella cheese or ¼ cup grated Parmesan cheese (optional)

1

In a large skillet combine red beans or kidney beans, undrained tomatoes, broth, uncooked brown rice, lima beans, green beans, and basil or Italian seasoning. Bring to boiling; reduce heat. Cover and simmer about 15 minutes or until rice is tender.

2

Stir in spaghetti sauce. Heat through. If desired, top with mozzarella or Parmesan cheese.

Nutrition Facts per serving: 259 calories, 4 g total fat, 0 mg cholesterol, 1,103 mg sodium, 50 g carbohydrate, 14 g protein.

CHRISTMAS LIMAS WITH PESTO BULGUR

Cook the dried beans a night or two ahead so you have them on hand to make this quick meal. If you prefer, skip cooking the beans and use the canned beans option.

Start to Finish: 20 minutes **Makes:** 4 servings

1$\frac{1}{3}$ **cups vegetable broth**
$\frac{2}{3}$ **cup bulgur**
2 **cups cooked dried Christmas lima beans, pinto beans, or cranberry beans,* or one 15-ounce can pinto beans, rinsed and drained**

1 **medium red sweet pepper, chopped**
$\frac{1}{4}$ **cup thinly sliced green onions**
$\frac{1}{3}$ **cup refrigerated pesto sauce**
Freshly ground black pepper
Toasted bread slices

1

In a medium saucepan bring broth to boiling; add bulgur. Return to boiling; reduce heat. Cover and simmer for 10 minutes. Remove from heat. Stir in beans, sweet pepper, green onions, and pesto sauce.

2

To serve, season bean mixture to taste with black pepper. Serve with toasted bread slices.

Nutrition Facts per serving: 419 calories, 13 g total fat, 5 mg cholesterol, 778 mg sodium, 65 g carbohydrate, 17 g protein.

*Note: To cook beans, rinse $\frac{3}{4}$ cup dried Christmas lima, pinto, or cranberry beans. In a large Dutch oven combine beans with 5 cups water. Bring to boiling; reduce heat. Simmer for 2 minutes. Remove from heat. Cover and let stand for 1 hour. (Or place beans in 5 cups cold water in a Dutch oven. Cover and let soak in a cool place overnight.) Drain and rinse beans. Return beans to pan. Add 5 cups fresh water. Bring to boiling; reduce heat. Cover and simmer for 1$\frac{1}{4}$ to 1$\frac{1}{2}$ hours or until tender. Drain.

SOUTHWESTERN BLACK BEAN CAKES WITH GUACAMOLE

These vegetarian burgers get a flavor boost from cilantro, chipotle pepper, and cumin.
(Pictured on page 91.)

Prep: 20 minutes **Grill:** 8 minutes **Makes:** 4 servings

½ of a medium avocado, seeded and
   peeled
1 tablespoon lime juice
   Salt
   Ground black pepper
2 slices whole wheat bread, torn
3 tablespoons fresh cilantro leaves
2 cloves garlic

1 15-ounce can black beans, rinsed
   and drained
1 canned chipotle pepper in adobo
   sauce
1 to 2 teaspoons adobo sauce
1 teaspoon ground cumin
1 beaten egg
1 small plum tomato, chopped

1

For guacamole, in a small bowl mash the avocado. Stir in lime juice; season to taste with salt and black pepper. Cover surface with plastic wrap and chill in the refrigerator until ready to serve.

2

Place torn bread in a food processor bowl or blender container. Cover and process or blend until bread resembles coarse crumbs. Transfer bread crumbs to a large bowl; set aside.

3

Place cilantro and garlic in the food processor bowl or blender container. Cover and process or blend until finely chopped. Add the beans, chipotle pepper, adobo sauce, and cumin. Cover and process or blend using on/off pulses until beans are coarsely chopped and mixture begins to pull away from the side of the bowl or container. Add mixture to bread crumbs. Add egg; mix well. Shape into four ½-inch patties.

4

Lightly grease the rack of an uncovered grill. Place patties on the rack. Grill directly over medium coals for 8 to 10 minutes or until patties are heated through, turning once halfway through grilling.

5

To serve, top patties with guacamole and tomato.

Nutrition Facts per serving: 178 calories, 7 g total fat, 53 mg cholesterol, 487 mg sodium, 25 g carbohydrate, 11 g protein.

MIXED BEAN AND PORTOBELLO RAGOUT

Two kinds of beans, chickpeas, and portobello mushrooms make this savory meatless medley as satisfying as any beef stew.

Start to Finish: 20 minutes **Makes:** 4 servings

1 10-ounce package frozen baby lima beans
1 cup fresh green beans cut into 1-inch pieces
1½ cups sliced and halved fresh portobello mushrooms or sliced button mushrooms (about 4 ounces)

1 tablespoon olive oil
1 tablespoon cold water
2 teaspoons cornstarch
1 14½-ounce can Cajun- or Italian-style stewed tomatoes
1 cup canned chickpeas (garbanzo beans), rinsed and drained

1

In a medium saucepan cook lima beans and green beans in boiling lightly salted water according to lima bean package directions. Drain.

2

Meanwhile, in a large skillet cook mushrooms in hot oil over medium heat for 5 minutes, stirring occasionally. In a small bowl combine the cold water and cornstarch; stir into mushrooms. Stir in undrained tomatoes and chickpeas. Cook and stir until thickened and bubbly. Cook and stir for 2 minutes more. Stir in cooked beans; heat through.

Nutrition Facts per serving: 214 calories, 5 g total fat, 0 mg cholesterol, 528 mg sodium, 36 g carbohydrate, 10 g protein.

JAPANESE-STYLE FRIED TOFU AND VEGETABLES

To assure that the tofu holds its shape when it is fried, be sure to get the extra-firm type. Look for it in your supermarket's produce or refrigerated section.

Prep: 25 minutes **Stand:** 1 hour **Cook:** 6 minutes **Makes:** 4 servings

- 1 10½-ounce package extra-firm light tofu (fresh bean curd), well drained
- 3 tablespoons reduced-sodium soy sauce
- 8 green onions
- 1 tablespoon toasted sesame oil
- 1 red sweet pepper, cut into thin, bite-size strips

- 1 yellow sweet pepper, cut into thin, bite-size strips
- 8 ounces fresh pea pods, cut in half lengthwise
- 2 tablespoons cornmeal
- 1 tablespoon white and/or black sesame seeds, toasted (optional)
- Thin green onion strips

1

Pat tofu dry with paper towels. Cut tofu crosswise into eight slices. Arrange slices in a single layer on a large plate or jelly-roll pan. Pour soy sauce over tofu; turn slices to coat. Let stand for 1 hour. Cut ends off green onions, leaving 3 inches of white and light green parts. Cut green onions in half lengthwise, forming 16 long strips.

2

In a large nonstick skillet heat toasted sesame oil over medium-high heat. Stir-fry peppers in hot oil for 1 minute. Add green onion strips and pea pods; stir-fry for 2 to 3 minutes more or until crisp-tender. Spoon cooked vegetables into a medium bowl. Set aside.

3

Drain tofu, reserving soy sauce. Stir reserved soy sauce into cooked vegetables; cover and keep warm. Carefully dip tofu slices in cornmeal to lightly coat both sides. Cook in the same skillet about 6 minutes or until crisp and hot, using a spatula to turn carefully halfway through cooking. (You may need to cook tofu slices in 2 batches; do not crowd skillet.)

4

To serve, arrange tofu slices over vegetables. If desired, sprinkle with sesame seeds and green onion strips.

Nutrition Facts per serving: 198 calories, 10 g total fat, 0 mg cholesterol, 410 mg sodium, 14 g carbohydrate, 16 g protein.

TOFU SKILLET LASAGNA

Slices of tofu replace traditional lasagna noodles in this stove-top version of the Italian classic.

Start to Finish: 25 minutes **Makes:** 4 servings

1 15$\frac{1}{2}$-ounce jar meatless spaghetti
    sauce with mushrooms (1$\frac{1}{2}$ cups)
8 to 10 ounces firm tofu (fresh bean
    curd), drained
3 cups loose-pack frozen broccoli,
    French-style green beans, onions,
    and red sweet peppers or other
    frozen vegetable combination

1 cup ricotta cheese
$\frac{1}{4}$ cup grated Parmesan cheese
    (1 ounce)
$\frac{1}{2}$ teaspoon dried oregano, crushed
$\frac{1}{4}$ teaspoon ground black pepper
$\frac{1}{2}$ cup shredded cheddar or mozzarella
    cheese (2 ounces)

1

In a large skillet heat 1$\frac{1}{4}$ cups of the spaghetti sauce over low heat. Thinly slice the tofu; arrange half of the slices in the skillet with sauce. Place frozen vegetables in a colander. Run cool water over the vegetables to thaw. Drain well to remove excess liquid. Sprinkle vegetables into skillet.

2

In a small bowl combine the ricotta cheese, Parmesan cheese, oregano, and black pepper. Drop by spoonfuls over vegetable mixture. Top with remaining tofu slices and remaining spaghetti sauce. Cover and cook over low heat for 10 to 15 minutes or until heated through. Sprinkle with cheddar or mozzarella cheese.

Nutrition Facts per serving: 369 calories, 19 g total fat, 32 mg cholesterol, 827 mg sodium, 27 g carbohydrate, 26 g protein.

COUSCOUS CAKES WITH BLACK BEAN SALSA

Is couscous a pasta or a grain? You decide. Technically it's made with ground semolina like some pastas, but it acts like a grain in this recipe and often substitutes for barley or bulgur.

Start to Finish: 20 minutes **Makes:** 4 servings

½ of a 15-ounce can (about ¾ cup) black beans, rinsed and drained
⅔ cup purchased corn relish
2 small plum tomatoes, chopped
1½ teaspoons lime juice
¼ teaspoon ground cumin
½ cup quick-cooking couscous

2 tablespoons whole wheat flour
½ teaspoon sugar
¼ teaspoon baking soda
⅛ teaspoon salt
¾ cup buttermilk or sour milk*
1 slightly beaten egg
1 tablespoon cooking oil

1

For salsa, in a medium bowl combine the beans, corn relish, tomatoes, lime juice, and cumin. Set aside.

2

In another medium bowl combine the uncooked couscous, whole wheat flour, sugar, baking soda, and salt. In a small bowl combine the buttermilk or sour milk, egg, and oil. Stir buttermilk mixture into flour mixture. Lightly grease a griddle or skillet; heat over medium heat. For each cake, spoon about 2 tablespoons of the batter onto the hot griddle or skillet. Cook for 4 to 6 minutes or until browned, turning to other sides when bottoms are lightly browned and edges are slightly dry.

3

To serve, spoon salsa mixture over cakes.

Nutrition Facts per serving: 255 calories, 4 g total fat, 2 mg cholesterol, 516 mg sodium, 46 g carbohydrate, 10 g protein.

*Note: To sour milk, place 2 teaspoons lemon juice or vinegar in a glass measuring cup. Add enough milk to make ¾ cup total liquid; stir. Let the mixture stand for 5 minutes before using it in recipe.

HOPPIN' JOHN VEGETABLE PILAF

*The main ingredients of the traditional Southern dish known as Hoppin' John—
black-eyed peas and rice—star in this colorful pilaf.*

Start to Finish: 25 minutes **Makes:** 4 servings

1 cup quick-cooking brown rice

1 medium carrot, thinly bias-sliced

$\frac{1}{2}$ cup sliced celery

2 green onions, sliced

4 cloves garlic, minced

1 tablespoon margarine or butter

1 15-ounce can black-eyed peas,
  rinsed and drained

1 11-ounce can whole kernel corn
  with sweet peppers

1 cup chopped seeded tomatoes

2 tablespoons snipped fresh parsley

1 tablespoon snipped fresh thyme or
  1 teaspoon dried thyme, crushed

2 teaspoons white wine
  Worcestershire sauce

$\frac{1}{4}$ to $\frac{1}{2}$ teaspoon crushed red pepper

$\frac{1}{8}$ teaspoon ground black pepper

1

Cook rice according to package directions, except omit any butter, margarine, or salt. Remove
from heat; set aside.

2

In a large skillet cook carrot, celery, green onions, and garlic in hot margarine or butter for 6 to
8 minutes or until crisp-tender, stirring occasionally. Add cooked rice, black-eyed peas, undrained corn,
and tomatoes; stir gently to mix. Cover and cook over low heat about 5 minutes or until heated
through, stirring occasionally. Stir in parsley, thyme, Worcestershire sauce, crushed red pepper, and
black pepper.

Nutrition Facts per serving: 286 calories, 5 g total fat, 0 mg cholesterol, 678 mg sodium, 54 g carbohydrate, 11 g protein.

LENTIL AND VEGGIE TOSTADAS

An assortment of vegetables and red lentils make these meatless tostadas tasty and colorful.

Start to Finish: 25 minutes   **Makes:** 4 servings

1³/₄ cups water
³/₄ cup dry red lentils, rinsed and
    drained
¹/₄ cup chopped onion
 1 to 2 tablespoons snipped fresh
    cilantro
¹/₂ teaspoon salt
¹/₂ teaspoon ground cumin

1 clove garlic, minced
4 tostada shells
2 cups assorted chopped fresh
    vegetables (such as broccoli,
    tomato, zucchini, and/or yellow
    summer squash)
³/₄ cup shredded Monterey Jack cheese
    (3 ounces)

1

In a medium saucepan stir together the water, lentils, onion, cilantro, salt, cumin, and garlic. Bring to boiling; reduce heat. Cover and simmer for 12 to 15 minutes or until lentils are tender and most of the liquid is absorbed. Use a fork to mash the cooked lentils.

2

Spread lentil mixture on tostada shells; top with vegetables and cheese. Place on a large baking sheet. Broil 3 to 4 inches from the heat about 2 minutes or until cheese melts.

Nutrition Facts per serving: 285 calories, 11 g total fat, 20 mg cholesterol, 526 mg sodium, 33 g carbohydrate, 16 g protein.

LENTIL-RICE PILAF

A quick stop at your supermarket's salad bar to pick up already prepared vegetables means you can have this Gouda-topped rice dish on the table in minutes.

Start to Finish: 20 minutes **Makes:** 4 servings

1/4 cup chopped onion
1/2 teaspoon bottled minced garlic
1 tablespoon olive oil
2 1/4 cups vegetable broth
1 cup quick-cooking brown rice
1/2 cup dry red lentils, rinsed and drained

1/4 teaspoon dried basil, crushed
4 cups salad bar vegetables cut into bite-size pieces (such as carrots, celery, broccoli, and red sweet pepper)
1/2 cup shredded smoked Gouda cheese (2 ounces)

1

In a medium saucepan cook onion and garlic in hot oil for 3 to 5 minutes or until onion is tender. Add broth, uncooked brown rice, lentils, and basil. Bring to boiling; reduce heat. Cover and simmer about 10 minutes or until lentils and rice are tender.

2

Meanwhile, in a covered medium saucepan cook salad bar vegetables in a small amount of boiling water for 4 to 6 minutes or until crisp-tender. Drain and keep warm.

3

To serve, top lentil-rice mixture with cooked vegetables. Sprinkle with Gouda cheese.

Nutrition Facts per serving: 263 calories, 9 g total fat, 16 mg cholesterol, 722 mg sodium, 37 g carbohydrate, 13 g protein.

PEPPERS STUFFED WITH CINNAMON BULGUR

Cinnamon gives these easy stovetop stuffed peppers a Middle Eastern accent.

Start to Finish: 30 minutes **Makes:** 4 servings

1 14-ounce can vegetable broth
½ cup shredded carrot
¼ cup chopped onion
3 inches stick cinnamon or dash ground cinnamon
⅛ teaspoon salt
¾ cup bulgur
⅓ cup dried cranberries or raisins

2 large or 4 small green, red, or yellow sweet peppers
¾ cup shredded Muenster, brick, or mozzarella cheese (3 ounces)
½ cup water
2 tablespoons sliced almonds or chopped pecans, toasted

1

In a large skillet combine broth, carrot, onion, cinnamon, and salt. Bring to boiling; reduce heat. Cover and simmer for 5 minutes. Stir in bulgur and cranberries or raisins. Remove from heat. Cover and let stand for 5 minutes; drain. If using stick cinnamon, remove from bulgur mixture.

2

Meanwhile, halve the sweet peppers lengthwise, removing seeds and membranes. Stir the cheese into bulgur mixture. Spoon into sweet pepper halves.

3

Place the sweet pepper halves, stuffed sides up, in skillet; add the water. Bring to boiling; reduce heat. Cover and simmer for 5 to 10 minutes or until sweet peppers are crisp-tender and bulgur mixture is heated through. Sprinkle with nuts.

Nutrition Facts per serving: 262 calories, 10 g total fat, 20 mg cholesterol, 633 mg sodium, 38 g carbohydrate, 11 g protein.

CREAMY BARLEY AND BROCCOLI

This risottolike dish gets its wonderful richness from Gruyère cheese.

Start to Finish: 25 minutes **Makes:** 4 servings

1 14-ounce can vegetable broth	Dash ground allspice
1 cup quick-cooking barley	1½ cups milk
2 cups broccoli florets	¾ cup shredded Gruyère cheese
2 tablespoons margarine or butter	(3 ounces)
2 tablespoons all-purpose flour	Cracked pink peppercorns
¼ teaspoon salt	

1

In a medium saucepan bring broth to boiling. Stir in barley. Return to boiling; reduce heat. Cover and simmer for 10 to 12 minutes or until barley is tender and most of the liquid is absorbed, adding broccoli the last 5 minutes of cooking.

2

Meanwhile, for sauce, in a small saucepan melt margarine or butter. Stir in flour, salt, and allspice. Add milk all at once. Cook and stir over medium heat until thickened and bubbly. Cook and stir for 1 minute more. Stir in ½ cup of the cheese until melted.

3

Gently stir the sauce into barley mixture. Divide the barley mixture among 4 dinner plates. Sprinkle with the remaining cheese and pink peppercorns.

Nutrition Facts per serving: 344 calories, 16 g total fat, 31 mg cholesterol, 757 mg sodium, 39 g carbohydrate, 16 g protein.

BULGUR-RICE PILAF WITH GREEN BEANS

Toasted nuts have a richer, fuller flavor than untoasted ones. In this recipe, just 2 tablespoons of almonds round out the flavor of this citrusy green bean pilaf.

Start to Finish: 25 minutes **Makes:** 4 servings

½ cup chopped onion
2 teaspoons cooking oil
1 14-ounce can vegetable broth
⅔ cup quick-cooking brown rice
⅔ cup bulgur
1 9-ounce package frozen French-cut
  green beans

¼ teaspoon finely shredded lemon
  peel
½ cup shredded reduced-fat cheddar
  cheese (2 ounces)
2 tablespoons sliced almonds, toasted
  Spiral-cut or coarsely shredded
  carrot (optional)

1

In a large saucepan cook onion in hot oil about 5 minutes or until onion is almost tender. Carefully add broth, uncooked brown rice, bulgur, and frozen beans. Bring to boiling; reduce heat. Cover and simmer about 15 minutes or until rice, bulgur, and beans are tender. Stir in lemon peel.

2

To serve, sprinkle cheese and almonds over rice mixture. If desired, garnish with carrot.

Nutrition Facts per serving: 229 calories, 8 g total fat, 10 mg cholesterol, 534 mg sodium, 34 g carbohydrate, 10 g protein.

HEARTY RICE SKILLET

Because these ingredients are easy to keep on hand, you can prepare this satisfying skillet meal whenever you have 25 minutes.

Start to Finish: 25 minutes **Makes:** 4 servings

1 15-ounce can black beans, chickpeas (garbanzo beans), or red kidney beans, rinsed and drained

1 14$\frac{1}{2}$-ounce can stewed tomatoes, cut up

2 cups loose-pack frozen mixed vegetables

1 cup water

$\frac{3}{4}$ cup quick-cooking brown rice

$\frac{1}{2}$ teaspoon dried thyme or dried dill, crushed

Several dashes bottled hot pepper sauce (optional)

1 10$\frac{3}{4}$-ounce can condensed tomato soup

$\frac{1}{3}$ cup slivered almonds, toasted

$\frac{1}{2}$ cup shredded mozzarella or cheddar cheese (2 ounces)

1

In a large skillet stir together beans or chickpeas, undrained tomatoes, frozen vegetables, the water, uncooked brown rice, thyme or dill, and, if desired, hot pepper sauce. Bring to boiling; reduce heat. Cover and simmer for 12 to 14 minutes or until rice is tender. Stir in soup; heat through.

2

To serve, stir in almonds and sprinkle with cheese.

Nutrition Facts per serving: 354 calories, 10 g total fat, 8 mg cholesterol, 1,244 mg sodium, 57 g carbohydrate, 19 g protein.

INDIAN-STYLE VEGETABLES AND RICE

Four different seasonings—curry powder, ginger, cardamom, and cinnamon—give this one-dish meal a taste of the Far East.

Start to Finish: 30 minutes **Makes:** 4 servings

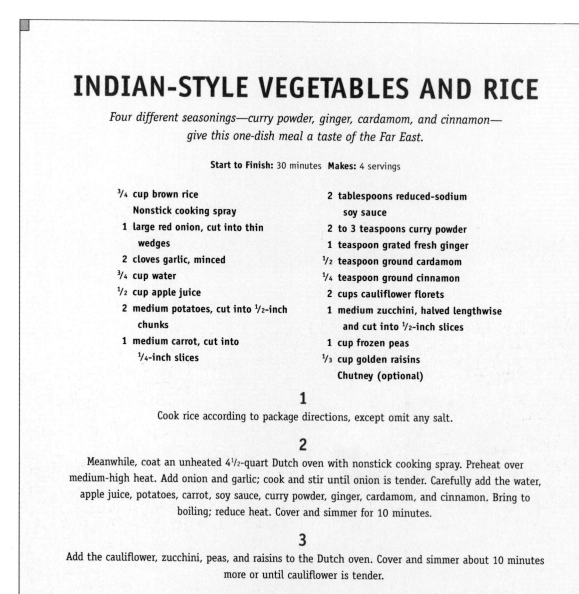

$3/4$ cup brown rice
Nonstick cooking spray
1 large red onion, cut into thin wedges
2 cloves garlic, minced
$3/4$ cup water
$1/2$ cup apple juice
2 medium potatoes, cut into $1/2$-inch chunks
1 medium carrot, cut into $1/4$-inch slices

2 tablespoons reduced-sodium soy sauce
2 to 3 teaspoons curry powder
1 teaspoon grated fresh ginger
$1/2$ teaspoon ground cardamom
$1/4$ teaspoon ground cinnamon
2 cups cauliflower florets
1 medium zucchini, halved lengthwise and cut into $1/2$-inch slices
1 cup frozen peas
$1/3$ cup golden raisins
Chutney (optional)

1

Cook rice according to package directions, except omit any salt.

2

Meanwhile, coat an unheated $4^{1}/_{2}$-quart Dutch oven with nonstick cooking spray. Preheat over medium-high heat. Add onion and garlic; cook and stir until onion is tender. Carefully add the water, apple juice, potatoes, carrot, soy sauce, curry powder, ginger, cardamom, and cinnamon. Bring to boiling; reduce heat. Cover and simmer for 10 minutes.

3

Add the cauliflower, zucchini, peas, and raisins to the Dutch oven. Cover and simmer about 10 minutes more or until cauliflower is tender.

4

To serve, spoon over the cooked rice. If desired, serve with chutney.

Nutrition Facts per serving: 330 calories, 2 g total fat, 0 mg cholesterol, 320 mg sodium, 72 g carbohydrate, 9 g protein.

RAREBIT SAUCE WITH ROASTED VEGETABLES

Roasted plum tomatoes add a slight tang and rich flavor to this creamy cheddar sauce.

Start to Finish: 30 minutes **Makes:** 6 servings

Cooking oil

12 plum tomatoes, cored and halved lengthwise

1 pound fresh asparagus, trimmed

2 tablespoons olive oil

Salt

Ground black pepper

³/₄ cup milk

1 tablespoon margarine or butter

2 beaten egg yolks

2 teaspoons Dijon-style mustard

Dash ground red pepper

10 ounces extra-sharp cheddar cheese, finely shredded (2¹/₂ cups)

6 thick slices sourdough bread, toasted

2 cloves garlic, peeled and halved

Fresh parsley sprigs

1

Line a 15×10×1-inch baking pan with foil; coat well with cooking oil. Place tomato halves, cut sides up, and asparagus spears on prepared pan. Drizzle with the olive oil; sprinkle lightly with salt and pepper. Roast, uncovered, in a 450°F oven for 8 to 15 minutes or until asparagus is crisp-tender and tomatoes are heated through.

2

Meanwhile, for sauce, in a medium saucepan heat milk and margarine or butter over medium heat. Gradually add hot milk mixture to egg yolks, stirring constantly. Stir in mustard and red pepper. Return mixture to saucepan. Continue to heat, stirring constantly, until mixture coats a metal spoon. Stir in cheese, a little at a time, stirring until melted after each addition. When all the cheese has been added, continue to heat and stir for 1 to 2 minutes more or until smooth (do not boil).

3

To serve, rub toast slices with the cut sides of garlic cloves. Transfer toast to serving plates, garlic sides up. Top each toast slice with 4 tomato halves and several of the asparagus spears. Spoon hot sauce over vegetables; top with parsley. Serve immediately.

Nutrition Facts per serving: 393 calories, 26 g total fat, 123 mg cholesterol, 539 mg sodium, 22 g carbohydrate, 19 g protein.

MUSHROOM AND BARLEY PILAF

This hearty main dish gets plenty of protein from the barley and pecans.

Start to Finish: 30 minutes **Makes:** 4 servings

2 cups sliced fresh mushrooms

4 green onions, sliced

1 medium carrot, shredded

½ teaspoon bottled minced garlic

1 tablespoon margarine or butter

1 14-ounce can vegetable broth or chicken broth

1½ cups quick-cooking barley

1 teaspoon dried basil, oregano, or marjoram, crushed, or ½ teaspoon dried sage, crushed

¼ teaspoon coarsely ground black pepper

1 6-ounce package frozen pea pods

½ cup pecan halves

1

In a medium saucepan cook the mushrooms, green onions, carrot, and garlic in hot margarine or butter over medium heat until mushrooms are tender. Stir in broth, barley, herb, and black pepper. Bring to boiling; reduce heat. Cover and simmer for 15 to 18 minutes or until barley is tender and liquid is absorbed.

2

Meanwhile, place frozen pea pods in a colander. Run cold water over the pea pods for 1 to 2 minutes or until thawed. Drain.

3

Stir pea pods into barley mixture. Cover and let stand for 2 to 3 minutes or until heated through. Top with pecans.

Nutrition Facts per serving: 414 calories, 14 g total fat, 0 mg cholesterol, 480 mg sodium, 67 g carbohydrate, 11 g protein.

VEGETABLE-TOPPED COUSCOUS

A colorful tomato sauce studded with chickpeas caps off mounds of fluffy couscous.

Start to Finish: 30 minutes **Makes:** 4 servings

1 large onion, cut into thin wedges
2 cloves garlic, minced
1 teaspoon olive oil or cooking oil
2 cups thinly sliced carrots
$1/2$ cup water
1 teaspoon dried basil, crushed
$1/2$ teaspoon ground cumin
$1/4$ teaspoon salt
$1/8$ teaspoon ground red pepper (optional)
2 medium zucchini, quartered lengthwise and cut into $1/2$-inch slices ($2^{1/2}$ cups)

1 15-ounce can chickpeas (garbanzo beans), rinsed and drained
1 $14^{1/2}$-ounce can low-sodium stewed tomatoes
2 tablespoons cold water
2 teaspoons cornstarch
2 cups vegetable broth
1 cup quick-cooking couscous
$1/4$ cup chopped unsalted dry-roasted peanuts

1

In a large saucepan cook onion and garlic in hot oil over medium-low heat until onion is crisp-tender. Stir in carrots, the $1/2$ cup water, the basil, cumin, salt, and, if desired, ground red pepper. Bring to boiling; reduce heat. Cover and simmer for 10 minutes.

2

Stir in zucchini, chickpeas, and undrained tomatoes. Cover and cook for 2 minutes. In a small bowl stir together the 2 tablespoons cold water and the cornstarch. Stir into tomato mixture. Cook and stir until thickened and bubbly. Cook and stir for 2 minutes more.

3

Meanwhile, in a medium saucepan bring broth to boiling. Remove from heat. Add couscous; cover and let stand about 5 minutes or until liquid is absorbed. Fluff with a fork.

4

To serve, spoon vegetable mixture over hot couscous. Sprinkle with peanuts.

Nutrition Facts per serving: 423 calories, 8 g total fat, 0 mg cholesterol, 892 mg sodium, 73 g carbohydrate, 16 g protein.

BROCCOLI RABE OVER POLENTA

Broccoli rabe is a slender cousin to broccoli, and its pungent flavor and crisp texture are an appealing counterpoint to delicate polenta in this meatless dish.

Start to Finish: 30 minutes **Makes:** 4 servings

1 cup quick-cooking polenta mix
1 cup vegetable broth
1 tablespoon cornstarch
1 cup chopped sweet onion (such as Vidalia or Walla Walla)
4 teaspoons olive oil
3 cloves garlic, minced

1 pound broccoli rabe, coarsely chopped (about 7 cups) or 3 cups coarsely chopped broccoli florets
$\frac{1}{2}$ of a 7-ounce jar roasted red sweet peppers, rinsed, drained, and chopped
$\frac{1}{4}$ cup pine nuts or slivered almonds, toasted

1

Prepare polenta according to package directions. Cover and keep warm. In a small bowl stir together broth and cornstarch. Set aside.

2

In a large skillet cook onion in hot oil over medium heat for 4 to 5 minutes or until tender. Add garlic; cook for 30 seconds more. Add broccoli rabe; cover and cook about 3 minutes or just until tender. (If using broccoli florets, cook and stir 3 to 4 minutes or until crisp-tender.) Stir in roasted sweet peppers.

3

Stir cornstarch mixture; add to vegetable mixture. Cook and stir until thickened and bubbly. Cook and stir for 2 minutes more.

4

To serve, divide polenta among 4 dinner plates. Spoon the vegetable mixture over polenta. Sprinkle with nuts.

Nutrition Facts per serving: 394 calories, 11 g total fat, 0 mg cholesterol, 256 mg sodium, 67 g carbohydrate, 12 g protein.

POLENTA WITH PORTOBELLO SAUCE

If you can't find a big portobello mushroom, buy smaller ones and halve before slicing.

Start to Finish: 25 minutes **Makes:** 2 servings

1 8-ounce fresh portobello mushroom, stem removed, quartered, and sliced (2½ cups)
½ cup finely chopped onion
3 cloves garlic, minced
1 tablespoon olive oil
2 tablespoons dry red wine
2 teaspoons snipped fresh oregano or ½ teaspoon dried oregano, crushed

3 plum tomatoes, chopped
1 cup water
⅓ cup cornmeal
1 tablespoon margarine or butter
⅛ teaspoon salt
⅓ cup shredded Havarti or brick cheese
Fresh oregano sprigs (optional)

1

In a large skillet cook and stir mushroom, onion, and garlic in hot oil over medium-high heat for 4 to 5 minutes or until mushroom is tender. Add the wine and, if using, dried oregano. Bring to boiling; reduce heat. Cover and simmer for 5 minutes to blend flavors. Stir in tomatoes and, if using, snipped fresh oregano; heat through. Remove from heat. Cover and keep warm.

2

Meanwhile, for polenta, in a small bowl stir together ½ cup of the water and the cornmeal; set aside. In a small saucepan bring the remaining water, the margarine or butter, and salt just to boiling. Slowly add the cornmeal mixture, stirring constantly. Reduce heat to low. Cook and stir about 10 minutes or until polenta is thick. Remove from heat. Stir in cheese.

3

To serve, divide the polenta between 2 shallow pasta bowls or soup bowls. Top with mushroom mixture. If desired, garnish with oregano sprigs.

Nutrition Facts per serving: 377 calories, 21 g total fat, 26 mg cholesterol, 345 mg sodium, 33 g carbohydrate, 12 g protein.

GINGERED VEGETABLE TOFU STIR-FRY

Extra firm tofu is sturdy enough to withstand the toss and tumble of stir-frying.
Look for it in the produce section of the supermarket.

Start to Finish: 25 minutes **Makes:** 4 servings

1 cup water

$1/4$ cup dry sherry or dry white wine

2 tablespoons soy sauce

4 teaspoons cornstarch

$1/2$ teaspoon sugar

1 tablespoon cooking oil

2 teaspoons grated fresh ginger

1 pound fresh asparagus, cut into
1-inch pieces (3 cups), or one
10-ounce package frozen cut
asparagus, thawed and well drained

1 small yellow summer squash, halved
lengthwise and sliced ($1^1/4$ cups)

2 green onions, sliced

1 $10^1/2$-ounce package extra firm tofu
(fresh bean curd), cut into $1/2$-inch
cubes

$1/2$ cup pine nuts or chopped almonds,
toasted

2 cups hot cooked brown rice

1

For sauce, in a small bowl stir together the water, dry sherry or white wine, soy sauce, cornstarch, and sugar. Set aside.

2

Pour oil into a wok or large skillet. Preheat the wok or large skillet over medium-high heat. Stir-fry the ginger in hot oil for 15 seconds. (Add more oil as necessary during cooking.) If using, add the fresh asparagus and the squash; stir-fry for 3 minutes. If using, add the thawed asparagus and the green onions; stir-fry about $1^1/2$ minutes more or until asparagus is crisp-tender. Remove vegetables from wok.

3

Add tofu to the hot wok or skillet. Carefully stir-fry for 2 to 3 minutes or until lightly browned. Remove from wok. Stir the sauce. Add sauce to hot wok. Cook and stir until thickened and bubbly. Return cooked vegetables and tofu to the wok. Stir to coat the ingredients with sauce. Cover and cook about 1 minute more or until heated through. Stir in nuts. Serve over hot cooked rice.

Nutrition Facts per serving: 412 calories, 21 g total fat, 0 mg cholesterol, 541 mg sodium, 38 g carbohydrate, 22 g protein.

FARM-STAND PAELLA

Fresh from the garden favorites make this meatless version of the Spanish classic one of the joys of summer.

Start to Finish: 25 minutes **Makes:** 4 servings

1 6-ounce jar marinated artichoke hearts

1 large onion, cut into wedges

4 cloves garlic, minced

2 14-ounce cans vegetable broth

$\frac{1}{3}$ cup water

$\frac{1}{2}$ teaspoon ground black pepper

$\frac{1}{4}$ teaspoon ground saffron

2 cups fresh green beans cut into 1-inch pieces

1 cup Arborio or long grain rice

2 fresh ears of corn, husked, cleaned, and cut crosswise into 2-inch pieces

2 medium zucchini, cut into $\frac{1}{2}$-inch slices

1 medium red sweet pepper, cut into thin, bite-size strips

$\frac{1}{2}$ teaspoon finely shredded lemon peel

1 15-ounce can chickpeas (garbanzo beans), rinsed and drained

1

Drain artichokes, reserving marinade. Set artichokes aside. In a 12-inch skillet heat reserved marinade over medium heat. Add onion and garlic. Cook, stirring frequently, for 5 minutes. Add broth, the water, black pepper, and saffron. Bring to boiling. Stir in green beans and uncooked rice. Return to boiling; reduce heat. Cover and simmer for 8 minutes.

2

Add corn, zucchini, sweet pepper, and lemon peel. Cover and cook for 7 to 8 minutes more or until vegetables and rice are tender. Stir in chickpeas and artichoke hearts; heat through.

Nutrition Facts per serving: 409 calories, 6 g total fat, 1 mg cholesterol, 1,125 mg sodium, 79 g carbohydrate, 14 g protein.

SUCCOTASH CUPS

Make these bean-and-corn-filled tortilla cups even more Tex-Mex by sprinkling on some shredded lettuce and a few sliced ripe olives. If you like, top everything off with a little sour cream.

Prep: 20 minutes **Bake:** 10 minutes **Makes:** 6 servings

1 10-ounce package frozen baby lima beans
1 10-ounce package frozen whole kernel corn
$\frac{1}{3}$ cup chopped onion
1 tablespoon margarine or butter
$\frac{3}{4}$ cup bottled salsa

Nonstick cooking spray
6 6-inch corn tortillas
$\frac{1}{2}$ cup shredded reduced-fat Monterey Jack or reduced-fat cheddar cheese (2 ounces)
1 small tomato, chopped

1

In a large covered saucepan cook beans in a small amount of boiling water for 8 minutes. Add corn and onion; cook 4 to 5 minutes more or until vegetables are tender. Drain well. Stir in the margarine or butter until melted. Stir in the salsa.

2

While vegetables are cooking, lightly coat six 10-ounce individual casseroles or custard cups with nonstick cooking spray. Place on shallow baking pan.

3

To soften the tortillas, wrap them in microwave-safe paper towels. Microwave on 100-percent (high) power for 15 to 20 seconds. (Or wrap tortillas in foil and heat in a 350°F oven for 10 minutes.) Gently press each tortilla into a prepared casserole or custard cup. Spoon some of the vegetable mixture into each tortilla cup; sprinkle with cheese. Bake in a 400°F oven about 10 minutes or until heated through. Top with chopped tomato.

Nutrition Facts per serving: 222 calories, 6 g total fat, 7 mg cholesterol, 254 mg sodium, 37 g carbohydrate, 10 g protein.

GARDEN BOUNTY COUSCOUS

The tiny semolina grains called couscous originated in North Africa. In fact, Moroccan cooks use them in so many ways that couscous appears at almost every meal.

Start to Finish: 30 minutes **Makes:** 4 servings

1 cup water

2 medium carrots, bias-sliced

1 medium onion, chopped

$\frac{1}{2}$ of a vegetable bouillon cube

$1\frac{1}{2}$ cups fresh pea pods, halved crosswise

1 $15\frac{1}{2}$-ounce can reduced-sodium chickpeas (garbanzo beans), rinsed and drained

1 cup quick-cooking couscous

$\frac{1}{2}$ cup fat-free milk

1 tablespoon snipped fresh savory or 1 teaspoon dried savory, crushed

$\frac{1}{4}$ teaspoon garlic powder

$\frac{1}{8}$ teaspoon ground black pepper

$\frac{1}{2}$ cup shredded reduced-fat Monterey Jack cheese (2 ounces)

1

In a medium saucepan combine the water, carrots, onion, and bouillon. Bring to boiling; reduce heat. Cover and simmer for 6 minutes. Stir in the pea pods. Cover and simmer about 3 minutes more or just until vegetables are crisp-tender.

2

Stir chickpeas, uncooked couscous, milk, savory, garlic powder, and pepper into vegetable mixture. Bring just to boiling. Remove from heat; cover and let stand for 5 minutes.

3

To serve, divide mixture among 4 dinner plates. Sprinkle with cheese.

Nutrition Facts per serving: 351 calories, 5 g total fat, 11 mg cholesterol, 468 mg sodium, 59 g carbohydrate, 18 g protein.

TOFU AND VEGETABLE STIR-FRY

Traditional Asian seasonings give this easy cook-and-stir meal flavor intrigue.

G 325
C 285

510 total

Start to Finish: 30 minutes **Makes:** 2 servings

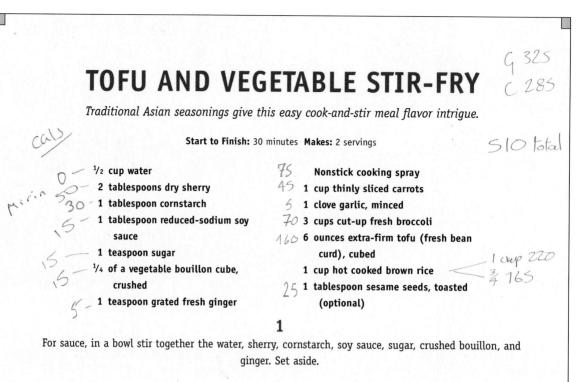

cals

Mirin 0 —
0 — ½ cup water
50 — 2 tablespoons dry sherry
30 — 1 tablespoon cornstarch
15 — 1 tablespoon reduced-sodium soy
     sauce
15 — 1 teaspoon sugar
15 — ¼ of a vegetable bouillon cube,
     crushed
5 — 1 teaspoon grated fresh ginger

75   Nonstick cooking spray
45   1 cup thinly sliced carrots
5   1 clove garlic, minced
70   3 cups cut-up fresh broccoli
160 6 ounces extra-firm tofu (fresh bean
     curd), cubed
     1 cup hot cooked brown rice   1 cup 220
                                    ¾ 165
25   1 tablespoon sesame seeds, toasted
     (optional)

1

For sauce, in a bowl stir together the water, sherry, cornstarch, soy sauce, sugar, crushed bouillon, and ginger. Set aside.

2

Coat an unheated wok or large skillet with nonstick cooking spray. Preheat over medium-high heat. Add carrots and garlic; stir-fry for 2 minutes. Add broccoli; stir-fry for 3 to 4 minutes more or until vegetables are crisp-tender. Push vegetables from center of wok.

3

Stir sauce; add to center of wok. Cook and stir until thickened and bubbly. Add tofu to wok. Stir all ingredients together to coat with sauce. Cook and stir for 1 minute.

4

To serve, spoon tofu mixture over hot cooked brown rice. If desired, sprinkle with sesame seeds.

Nutrition Facts per serving: 305 calories, 6 g total fat, 0 mg cholesterol, 584 mg sodium, 48 g carbohydrate, 16 g protein.

VEGGIE SKILLET

For an extra flavor bonus, replace a cup of the spaghetti sauce with a cup of salsa.

Start to Finish: 20 minutes **Makes:** 4 servings

3 cups loose-pack frozen diced hash
   brown potatoes with onions and
   peppers
2 tablespoons cooking oil
2 cups bottled meatless spaghetti
   sauce with mushrooms

1 cup loose-pack frozen peas and
   carrots
1 cup loose-pack frozen whole kernel
   corn
$\frac{1}{2}$ cup shredded cheddar cheese or
   mozzarella cheese (2 ounces)

1

In a large skillet cook potatoes in hot oil over medium heat for 6 to 8 minutes or until nearly tender,
stirring occasionally.

2

Stir spaghetti sauce, peas and carrots, and corn into potatoes in the skillet. Bring to boiling; reduce
heat. Cover and simmer for 5 to 7 minutes or until vegetables are tender. Sprinkle with cheese. Cover
and let stand about 1 minute or until cheese starts to melt.

Nutrition Facts per serving: 406 calories, 21 g total fat, 20 mg cholesterol, 742 mg sodium, 49 g carbohydrate, 10 g protein.

CORN WAFFLES WITH TOMATO SALSA

These unique waffles are so easy because they start with a corn muffin mix.
They're perfect for topping with the sassy bean salsa.

Start to Finish: 30 minutes **Makes:** 4 servings

6 plum tomatoes, halved
2 teaspoons olive oil
1 15-ounce can black beans or small
   white beans, rinsed and drained
⅓ cup sliced green onions
2 tablespoons snipped fresh cilantro
   or parsley
2 tablespoons lime juice

1 to 2 fresh serrano peppers,*
   chopped
¼ teaspoon salt
1 8½-ounce package corn muffin mix
½ cup fresh or frozen whole kernel
   corn
¼ cup plain fat-free yogurt
   Fresh cilantro sprigs (optional)

1

For salsa, brush tomato halves with 1 teaspoon of the oil; place on the unheated rack of a broiler pan. Broil 4 to 5 inches from the heat for 8 to 10 minutes or until tomatoes begin to char, turning once halfway through broiling. Remove from broiler pan and cool slightly; coarsely chop.

2

Meanwhile, in a medium bowl combine the remaining olive oil, the beans, green onions, snipped cilantro or parsley, lime juice, serrano peppers, and salt. Stir in tomatoes and any juices. Set aside.

3

For waffles, prepare corn muffin mix according to package directions, except stir corn into batter. (If necessary, add an additional 1 to 2 tablespoons milk to thin batter.)

4

Lightly grease waffle baker; preheat. Pour about half of the batter onto the grid of hot waffle baker. Close lid quickly; do not open until done. Bake according to manufacturer's directions. When done, use a fork to lift waffle off grid; keep warm. Repeat with remaining batter.

5

To serve, cut waffles in half. Divide warm waffles among 4 dinner plates. Top with salsa and yogurt. If desired, garnish with cilantro sprigs.

Nutrition Facts per serving: 417 calories, 12 g total fat, 55 mg cholesterol, 841 mg sodium, 70 g carbohydrate, 15 g protein.

*Note: Because chile peppers, such as serranos, contain volatile oils that can burn your skin and eyes, avoid direct contact with them as much as possible. When working with chile peppers, wear plastic or rubber gloves. If your bare hands do touch the chile peppers, wash your hands and nails well with soap and warm water.

CURRIED VEGETABLE STIR-FRY

Brussels sprouts give this hearty stir-fry a European accent.

Start to Finish: 30 minutes **Makes:** 4 servings

2 cups water
1¼ cups quick-cooking barley
1 cup fresh Brussels sprouts or frozen
   Brussels sprouts, thawed
1 cup cold water
4 teaspoons cornstarch
1 to 2 teaspoons curry powder
½ of a vegetable bouillon cube,
   crushed
Nonstick cooking spray

1½ cups red, yellow, and/or green sweet
   pepper strips
2 tablespoons thinly sliced green
   onion
1 cup bias-sliced carrots
4 ounces extra-firm light tofu (fresh
   bean curd), cut into ½-inch cubes
   (optional)
¼ cup peanuts

1

In a medium saucepan bring the 2 cups water to boiling. Slowly add the barley. Return to boiling; reduce heat. Cover and simmer for 10 to 12 minutes or until barley is tender. If necessary, drain thoroughly.

2

Meanwhile, cut Brussels sprouts in half. In a small saucepan cook Brussels sprouts in a small amount of boiling water for 3 minutes. Drain well. For sauce, in a small bowl stir together the 1 cup cold water, the cornstarch, curry powder, and bouillon. Set aside.

3

Coat an unheated wok or large skillet with nonstick cooking spray. Preheat over medium-high heat. Add sweet peppers and green onion. Stir-fry for 1 minute. Add the Brussels sprouts and carrots. Stir-fry for 3 minutes more. Push the vegetables from center of wok. Stir sauce; add to the center of wok. Cook and stir until thickened and bubbly. Stir to coat all ingredients with sauce. Cook and stir for 1 minute. If desired, stir in tofu; cover and cook about 30 seconds or until heated through. Serve immediately over hot cooked barley. Sprinkle with peanuts.

Nutrition Facts per serving: 320 calories, 6 g total fat, 0 mg cholesterol, 333 mg sodium, 59 g carbohydrate, 10 g protein.

SOUPS

If a soup supper seems like a perfect way to top off the day, ladle up one of these meatless medleys.

Hearty Bean and Rice Soup
(see recipe, page 152)

CHUNKY POTATO-PEPPER SOUP

For a milder version of this sassy soup, reduce or omit the ground red pepper.

Start to Finish: 30 minutes **Makes:** 4 servings

3 medium potatoes, cubed
2 cups vegetable broth
1 small green sweet pepper, chopped
1 small red sweet pepper, chopped
1 small yellow sweet pepper, chopped
1 small onion, chopped

¼ cup margarine or butter
¼ cup all-purpose flour
¼ teaspoon salt
¼ teaspoon ground black pepper
⅛ teaspoon ground red pepper
3 cups milk

1

In a medium saucepan combine potatoes and broth. Bring to boiling; reduce heat. Cover and simmer about 10 minutes or until potatoes are tender. Do not drain.

2

Meanwhile, in a large saucepan cook the green sweet pepper, red sweet pepper, yellow sweet pepper, and onion in hot margarine or butter until tender. Stir in flour, salt, black pepper, and ground red pepper. Add milk all at once. Cook and stir until thickened and bubbly. Cook and stir for 1 minute more. Stir in undrained potatoes. Heat through.

3

To serve, ladle soup into bowls.

Nutrition Facts per serving: 344 calories, 16 g total fat, 14 mg cholesterol, 752 mg sodium, 39 g carbohydrate, 12 g protein.

HEARTY BEAN AND RICE SOUP

Italian risottos made with short, plump grains of Arborio rice are known for their creamy textures. Arborio rice adds the same quality to this vegetable and bean meal in a bowl.
(Pictured on page 149.)

Start to Finish: 30 minutes **Makes:** 6 servings

2 stalks celery, chopped
1 large onion, chopped
2 cloves garlic, minced
1 tablespoon olive oil
5 cups vegetable broth
1 cup water
½ cup Arborio rice or long grain rice
6 cups torn fresh spinach

3 medium tomatoes, chopped
1 medium zucchini, coarsely chopped
1 15-ounce can Great Northern beans, rinsed and drained
¼ cup snipped fresh thyme
¼ teaspoon cracked black pepper
½ cup crumbled feta cheese (2 ounces)
Fresh spinach leaves (optional)

1

In a Dutch oven cook celery, onion, and garlic in hot oil until tender. Add broth, the water, and the uncooked rice. Bring to boiling; reduce heat. Cover and simmer for 15 minutes.

2

Stir torn spinach, tomatoes, zucchini, beans, thyme, and pepper into mixture in Dutch oven. Cook and stir until heated through.

3

To serve, ladle soup into bowls. Top with feta cheese. If desired, garnish with spinach leaves.

Nutrition Facts per serving: 252 calories, 6 g total fat, 8 mg cholesterol, 834 mg sodium, 39 g carbohydrate, 13 g protein.

PEANUT BUTTER-VEGETABLE SOUP

Peanut butter not only adds protein to this all-vegetable stew, it also helps create a velvety smooth texture.

Start to Finish: 25 minutes **Makes:** 4 servings

3 stalks celery, sliced

3 medium carrots, chopped

1 large onion, chopped

3 cloves garlic, minced

2 tablespoons margarine or butter

3 cups water

1 medium potato, diced

1 medium zucchini, sliced

2 vegetable bouillon cubes

$1/2$ teaspoon ground black pepper

1 16-ounce can tomatoes, cut up

2 tablespoons snipped fresh parsley

$1/2$ cup peanut butter

1

In a covered large saucepan or Dutch oven cook celery, carrots, onion, and garlic in hot margarine or butter about 5 minutes or until onion is tender. Stir in the water, potato, zucchini, bouillon, and pepper. Bring to boiling; reduce heat. Cover and simmer for 10 minutes. Stir in undrained tomatoes and parsley.

2

Place peanut butter in a small bowl; gradually add about 1 cup of the hot tomato mixture, stirring until smooth. Stir peanut butter mixture into remaining tomato mixture in saucepan. Cook and stir until heated through.

3

To serve, ladle soup into bowls.

Nutrition Facts per serving: 348 calories, 23 g total fat, 0 mg cholesterol, 1,385 mg sodium, 31 g carbohydrate, 12 g protein.

CHEESE SOUP WITH JALAPEÑO PESTO

*A unique pesto made from cilantro, parsley, and jalapeño pepper makes
this a lively cheese soup like no other.*

Start to Finish: 30 minutes **Makes:** 5 servings

3 cups vegetable broth

1¹/₂ cups shredded carrot

1 cup chopped green onions

¹/₄ cup tomato paste

2¹/₂ cups milk

¹/₄ cup all-purpose flour

1 teaspoon dry mustard

¹/₄ teaspoon ground black pepper

2 3-ounce packages cream cheese, cut
into cubes and softened

3 cups shredded sharp cheddar or
American cheese (12 ounces)

1 recipe Jalapeño Pesto

1

In a large saucepan combine broth, carrot, green onions, and tomato paste. Bring to boiling; reduce heat. Cover and simmer for 2 minutes. In a medium bowl combine milk, flour, dry mustard, and black pepper; stir into broth mixture. Cook and stir over medium heat until thickened and bubbly. Cook and stir for 1 minute more.

2

Place cream cheese in a small bowl; stir in about 1 cup of the hot milk mixture, stirring until smooth. Stir cream cheese mixture into remaining milk mixture in saucepan. Stir in cheddar or American cheese until melted.

3

To serve, spoon soup into bowls. Spoon about 1 tablespoon Jalapeño Pesto onto each serving.

Jalapeño Pesto: In a blender container or food processor bowl combine ¹/₄ cup firmly packed fresh cilantro leaves; ¹/₄ cup firmly packed fresh parsley sprigs with stems removed; 3 tablespoons grated Parmesan cheese; 2 tablespoons olive oil or cooking oil; ¹/₄ teaspoon finely shredded lime peel; 1 teaspoon lime juice; 2 fresh jalapeño peppers,* cut up; and 1 clove garlic, minced. Cover and blend or process until a paste forms. Cover and chill in the refrigerator until serving time or up to 2 days. Makes about ¹/₃ cup.

Nutrition Facts per serving: 588 calories, 44 g total fat, 121 mg cholesterol, 1,361 mg sodium, 23 g carbohydrate, 28 g protein.

*Note: Because chile peppers, such as jalapeños, contain volatile oils that can burn your skin and eyes, avoid direct contact with them as much as possible. When working with chile peppers, wear plastic or rubber gloves. If your bare hands do touch the chile peppers, wash your hands and nails well with soap and warm water.

Soups

CORN AND GREEN CHILE CHOWDER

To use fresh corn in place of the frozen, cut the kernels from 2 medium ears of corn.

Start to Finish: 25 minutes   **Makes:** 3 servings

- 1 medium onion, chopped
- 2 tablespoons margarine or butter
- 2 tablespoons all-purpose flour
- 2 cups water
- 1 large potato, peeled and diced
- 1 10-ounce package frozen whole kernel corn
- 1 4-ounce can diced green chile peppers
- 1½ vegetable bouillon cubes

- ¼ teaspoon coarsely ground black pepper
- 2 cups milk
- 2 tablespoons snipped fresh cilantro or parsley
- Fresh cilantro or parsley sprigs (optional)
- Sliced fresh chile peppers* (optional)

1

In a large saucepan cook onion in hot margarine or butter until tender. Stir in flour. Add the water, potato, corn, diced green chile peppers, bouillon, and black pepper. Bring to boiling; reduce heat. Cover and simmer about 10 minutes or until potatoes are tender. Stir in the milk and snipped cilantro or parsley; heat through.

2

To serve, ladle chowder into bowls. If desired, garnish each serving with cilantro or parsley sprigs and sliced fresh chile peppers.

Nutrition Facts per serving: 323 calories, 12 g total fat, 12 mg cholesterol, 779 mg sodium, 47 g carbohydrate, 11 g protein.

*Note: Because chile peppers contain volatile oils that can burn your skin and eyes, avoid direct contact with them as much as possible. When working with chile peppers, wear plastic or rubber gloves. If your bare hands do touch the chile peppers, wash your hands and nails well with soap and warm water.

CREAMY CARROT AND PASTA SOUP

The hot Jamaican spices in this creamy pasta soup dance in your mouth.

Start to Finish: 30 minutes **Makes:** 4 servings

2 14-ounce cans vegetable broth or
  chicken broth
2 cups sliced carrots
1 large potato, peeled and diced
1 cup chopped onion
1 tablespoon grated fresh ginger

$^{1}/_{2}$ to 1 teaspoon Jamaican jerk
  seasoning
8 ounces dried radiatore or rotini
$1^{1}/_{2}$ cups milk or one 12-ounce can
  evaporated fat-free milk
Fresh chives (optional)

1

In a large saucepan combine broth, carrots, potato, onion, ginger, and Jamaican jerk seasoning.
Bring to boiling; reduce heat. Cover and simmer for 15 to 20 minutes or until vegetables are very
tender. Cool slightly.

2

Meanwhile, cook pasta according to package directions. Drain.

3

Place one-fourth of the vegetable mixture in a food processor bowl. Cover and process until smooth.
Transfer vegetable mixture to a bowl. Repeat 3 times more. Return all to saucepan. Stir in pasta and
milk; heat through. Ladle soup into bowls. If desired, top with chives.

Nutrition Facts per serving: 351 calories, 4 g total fat, 7 mg cholesterol, 937 mg sodium, 67 g carbohydrate, 14 g protein.

TUNISIAN VEGETABLE CHILI

White beans, such as Great Northern and white kidney, give this stew a more subtle flavor than traditional chili.

Start to Finish: 25 minutes **Makes:** 4 servings

Nonstick cooking spray
1 medium onion, chopped
1 medium carrot, sliced
1 small yellow or green sweet pepper, cut into ¹/₂-inch pieces
1 15-ounce can Great Northern beans, white kidney beans (cannellini beans), or pinto beans, rinsed and drained
1 14¹/₂-ounce can diced tomatoes

¹/₂ cup apple juice or apple cider
¹/₃ cup raisins
2 teaspoons chili powder
³/₄ teaspoon ground cinnamon
¹/₄ teaspoon salt
Several dashes bottled hot pepper sauce
2 cups hot cooked couscous
¹/₄ cup finely chopped peanuts (optional)

1

Coat an unheated medium saucepan with nonstick cooking spray. Preheat over medium-low heat. Add onion, carrot, and sweet pepper; cook for 8 to 10 minutes or just until vegetables are tender, stirring occasionally.

2

Add beans, undrained tomatoes, apple juice or cider, raisins, chili powder, cinnamon, salt, and hot pepper sauce. Bring to boiling; reduce heat. Cover and simmer for 5 minutes, stirring occasionally.

3

To serve, ladle couscous and chili into bowls. If desired, garnish with peanuts.

Nutrition Facts per serving: 261 calories, 1 g total fat, 0 mg cholesterol, 581 mg sodium, 59 g carbohydrate, 12 g protein.

VEGETARIAN CHILI

*Three different beans plus corn and summer squash make this
beer-seasoned chili a sure-fire favorite.*

Start to Finish: 40 minutes **Makes:** 6 servings

3 cloves garlic, minced
1 tablespoon cooking oil
2 14¹/₂-ounce cans chunky chili-style
   tomatoes or low-sodium stewed
   tomatoes
1 12-ounce can beer or nonalcoholic
   beer
1 cup water
1 8-ounce can low-sodium tomato
   sauce
3 to 4 teaspoons chili powder
1 tablespoon snipped fresh oregano or
   1 teaspoon dried oregano, crushed
1 tablespoon Dijon-style mustard
1 teaspoon ground cumin
¹/₂ teaspoon ground black pepper

Several dashes bottled hot pepper
   sauce (optional)
1 15-ounce can reduced-sodium pinto
   beans, rinsed and drained
1 15-ounce can white kidney beans
   (cannellini beans), rinsed and
   drained
1 15-ounce can reduced-sodium red
   kidney beans, rinsed and drained
1¹/₂ cups fresh or frozen whole kernel
   corn
1¹/₂ cups chopped zucchini or yellow
   summer squash
³/₄ cup shredded cheddar or Monterey
   Jack cheese (3 ounces) (optional)

1

In a 4-quart Dutch oven cook garlic in hot oil for 30 seconds. Stir in the undrained tomatoes, beer, the
water, tomato sauce, chili powder, oregano, mustard, cumin, black pepper, and, if desired, hot pepper
sauce. Stir in pinto beans, white kidney beans, and red kidney beans. Bring to boiling; reduce heat.
Cover and simmer for 10 minutes.

2

Stir in corn and zucchini or yellow summer squash. Return to boiling; reduce heat. Cover and simmer
about 10 minutes more or until vegetables are tender.

3

To serve, ladle chili into bowls. If desired, top with shredded cheese.

Nutrition Facts per serving: 256 calories, 4 g total fat, 0 mg cholesterol, 1,006 mg sodium, 54 g carbohydrate, 15 g protein.

VEGETARIAN SKILLET CHILI

This mild family-style chili gets a hint of fire from the chili powder and chopped tomatoes and green chile peppers.

Start to Finish: 30 minutes **Makes:** 4 servings

1 cup chopped onion

2 tablespoons olive oil

2 teaspoons chili powder

1 teaspoon cumin

2 10-ounce cans chopped tomatoes
  and green chile peppers

1 large sweet potato, peeled and
  chopped

2 15-ounce cans black beans, rinsed
  and drained

1 large zucchini, chopped
  Fresh chile peppers (optional)

1

In a 12-inch skillet cook onion in hot oil until lightly browned. Stir in chili powder and cumin; cook for 1 minute. Add tomatoes and green chile peppers and sweet potato. Bring to boiling; reduce heat. Cover and simmer about 6 minutes or until sweet potato is partially cooked.

2

Add beans and zucchini; cook just until zucchini is tender.

3

To serve, ladle chili into bowls. If desired, garnish with fresh chile peppers.

Nutrition Facts per serving: 300 calories, 9 g total fat, 0 mg cholesterol, 1,020 mg sodium, 44 g carbohydrate, 12 g protein.

WHITE BEAN AND PASTA SOUP

For a satisfying supper, serve this thyme-flavored soup with a spinach salad and crusty French or Italian bread.

Start to Finish: 35 minutes **Makes:** 4 or 5 servings

2 cups vegetable broth or chicken broth

2 medium carrots, chopped

1 medium onion, chopped

1 stalk celery, sliced

$\frac{1}{8}$ teaspoon ground white pepper (optional)

1 cup dried radiatore or mostaccioli

2 cups milk

3 tablespoons all-purpose flour

1 15-ounce can Great Northern or white kidney (cannellini) beans, drained and rinsed

1 tablespoon snipped fresh thyme

1 cup chopped tomato

1

In a large saucepan combine broth, carrots, onion, celery, and, if desired, white pepper. Bring to boiling; stir in pasta. Return to boiling; reduce heat. Cover and simmer for 10 to 12 minutes or until pasta is tender but still firm.

2

Meanwhile, in a small bowl gradually stir milk into flour until smooth. Stir milk-flour mixture into pasta mixture. Cook and stir over medium heat until thickened and bubbly. Cook and stir for 2 minutes more. Stir in beans and thyme; heat through. Top with tomato.

Nutrition Facts per serving: 340 calories, 4 g total fat, 10 mg cholesterol, 970 mg sodium, 56 g carbohydrate, 19 g protein.

BEER AND CHEESE SOUP

Add crunch to this creamy, full-bodied soup by topping it with a toast triangle or croutons.

Start to Finish: 30 minutes **Makes:** 6 servings

2 cups sliced fresh mushrooms
1½ cups chopped carrots
1 cup water
¾ cup chopped red or green sweet pepper
¾ cup chopped onion
2½ cups fat-free milk

⅓ cup all-purpose flour
¼ teaspoon ground white pepper
½ cup beer
8 ounces light processed cheese product, cubed, or 2 cups shredded reduced-fat sharp cheddar cheese (8 ounces)

1

In a large saucepan combine mushrooms, carrots, the water, sweet pepper, and onion. Bring to boiling; reduce heat. Cover and simmer for 3 to 4 minutes or just until vegetables are tender. (Do not drain.)

2

Meanwhile, in a screw-top jar shake together 1 cup of the milk and the flour. Add milk-flour mixture to vegetables in saucepan. Stir in the remaining milk and the white pepper. Cook and stir until thickened and bubbly. Cook and stir for 1 minute more. Stir in the beer; heat through. Reduce heat. Stir in cheese until melted.

Nutrition Facts per serving: 180 calories, 5 g total fat, 15 mg cholesterol, 658 mg sodium, 22 g carbohydrate, 12 g protein.

AUTUMN BEAN AND BRUSSELS SPROUTS STEW

Apple and winter squash help mellow the flavor of this hearty cold-weather tempter.

Start to Finish: 30 minutes **Makes:** 4 to 6 servings

Nonstick cooking spray
1 small onion, chopped
6 cloves garlic, minced
1 small fennel bulb, trimmed, cored, and thinly sliced (about 2 cups)
12 ounces acorn, butternut, or turban squash, seeded, peeled, and cut into ³/₄-inch pieces (about 2 cups)
8 ounces fresh Brussels sprouts, trimmed and halved (2 cups)
1 14-ounce can vegetable broth
¹/₃ cup dry white wine or apple juice
2 tablespoons snipped fresh sage or 1 teaspoon dried sage, crushed

1 tablespoon snipped fresh rosemary or 1 teaspoon dried rosemary, crushed
1 medium tart apple, cored and coarsely chopped (about 1 cup) or 6 dried apricots, quartered
1 15-ounce can red kidney beans, rinsed and drained
1 tablespoon sherry vinegar or balsamic vinegar
1 tablespoon honey
Salt
Ground black pepper

1

Lightly coat an unheated 4-quart Dutch oven with nonstick cooking spray. Preheat Dutch oven over medium heat. Add onion and garlic to Dutch oven; cook and stir for 5 minutes. Add fennel, squash, Brussels sprouts, broth, wine or apple juice, sage, and rosemary. Bring to boiling; reduce heat. Cover and simmer about 8 minutes or until vegetables are almost tender.

2

Add apple or apricots. Cover and cook about 3 minutes more or just until sprouts are tender. Add beans, vinegar, and honey; heat through. Season to taste with salt and pepper.

3

To serve, ladle stew into bowls.

Nutrition Facts per serving: 201 calories, 1 g total fat, 0 mg cholesterol, 690 mg sodium, 44 g carbohydrate, 11 g protein.

CHICKPEA STEW

Pick up a loaf of your favorite crusty bread to serve along with this chock-full-of-vegetables stew.

Start to Finish: 20 minutes **Makes:** 4 servings

- 1 large onion, chopped
- 1 medium green sweet pepper, chopped
- 3 cloves garlic, minced
- 2 teaspoons cooking oil
- 1½ teaspoons ground cumin
- ½ teaspoon paprika
- ⅛ to ¼ teaspoon ground red pepper
- 2 cups vegetable broth
- 1½ cups water

- 1 10-ounce package frozen whole kernel corn
- 2 tablespoons snipped fresh oregano
- 1 15-ounce can chickpeas (garbanzo beans), rinsed and drained
- 1 medium tomato, chopped
- 2 tablespoons lemon juice
- ¼ cup crumbled feta cheese (1 ounce)
- 2 tablespoons sliced green onion

1

In a large saucepan cook onion, sweet pepper, and garlic in hot oil until onion is tender, stirring occasionally. Stir in cumin, paprika, and ground red pepper; cook for 1 minute more.

2

Carefully add broth, the water, frozen corn, and oregano. Bring to boiling; reduce heat. Cover and simmer for 5 to 10 minutes or until corn is tender. Stir in chickpeas, tomato, and lemon juice. Heat through.

3

To serve, ladle stew into bowls. Sprinkle with feta cheese and green onion.

Nutrition Facts per serving: 239 calories, 7 g total fat, 6 mg cholesterol, 886 mg sodium, 41 g carbohydrate, 10 g protein.

TORTELLINI-PESTO SOUP WITH VEGETABLES

You'll usually find bottled pesto in your supermarket's produce section or in the Italian-food aisle.

Start to Finish: 25 minutes **Makes:** 4 servings

1 small onion, chopped

2 cloves garlic, minced

1 tablespoon margarine or butter

5 cups vegetable broth

2 cups loose-pack frozen broccoli, cauliflower, and carrot or other frozen vegetable combination

1 9-ounce package refrigerated cheese-filled tortellini

¼ cup purchased pesto

¼ cup shredded Parmesan cheese (1 ounce)

1

In a large saucepan cook onion and garlic in hot margarine or butter until tender. Stir in broth and frozen vegetables. Bring to boiling. Stir in tortellini. Return to boiling; reduce heat. Cover and simmer about 8 minutes or until tortellini is tender but still firm and vegetables are crisp-tender. Stir in pesto.

2

To serve, ladle soup into bowls. Sprinkle with Parmesan cheese.

Nutrition Facts per serving: 414 calories, 19 g total fat, 42 mg cholesterol, 1,742 mg sodium, 51 g carbohydrate, 18 g protein.

PROVENÇAL VEGETABLE STEW

This captivating meatless stew showcases olive oil, tomatoes, and eggplant, as do many favorites from the Provençal region of France.

Start to Finish: 30 minutes **Makes:** 4 servings

- 2 teaspoons olive oil
- 4 ¹/₂-inch slices baguette-style French bread
- 2 tablespoons grated Romano or Parmesan cheese
- 2 baby eggplants or 1 very small eggplant (about 8 ounces)
- 1 large zucchini, quartered lengthwise
- 1 large yellow summer squash or crookneck squash, quartered lengthwise
- 4 cloves garlic, minced
- 4 teaspoons olive oil
- 1 14-ounce can vegetable broth

- 1 15- or 16-ounce can white kidney beans (cannellini beans) or Great Northern beans, rinsed and drained
- 1 large tomato, chopped
- 1 tablespoon snipped fresh basil
- 2 teaspoons snipped fresh rosemary or thyme
- ¹/₄ teaspoon freshly ground black pepper
- 1 tablespoon white balsamic vinegar or balsamic vinegar
- 2 tablespoons grated Romano or Parmesan cheese
- Fresh basil sprigs (optional)

1
For croutons, lightly brush the 2 teaspoons oil over 1 side of each bread slice. Sprinkle with 2 tablespoons cheese. Arrange bread, cheese sides up, on a baking sheet; bake in a 400°F oven for 8 to 9 minutes or until toasted. Set aside. Meanwhile, peel eggplants, if desired; cut into ³/₄-inch cubes. Slice zucchini and yellow summer squash into ¹/₂-inch slices.

2
In a large saucepan cook and stir eggplant, squash, and garlic in the 4 teaspoons hot oil for 5 minutes. Add broth. Bring to boiling; reduce heat. Simmer, uncovered, for 5 minutes more. Stir in beans. Simmer, uncovered, for 2 to 3 minutes more or until vegetables are tender. Stir in tomato, snipped basil, rosemary or thyme, and pepper; heat through.

3
To serve, remove from heat; stir in vinegar. Ladle stew into bowls. Top with croutons and sprinkle with 2 tablespoons cheese. If desired, garnish with basil sprigs.

Nutrition Facts per serving: 261 calories, 11 g total fat, 5 mg cholesterol, 861 mg sodium, 39 g carbohydrate, 12 g protein.

TEX-MEX CHILI WITH DUMPLINGS

Dress up each serving of this hearty chili with a garnish of lime wedges and sliced carambola (star fruit).

Start to Finish: 30 minutes **Makes:** 5 servings

¹⁄₃ cup all-purpose flour	1 15-ounce can chickpeas (garbanzo
¹⁄₃ cup yellow cornmeal	beans), rinsed and drained
1 teaspoon baking powder	1 15-ounce can red kidney beans,
¹⁄₄ teaspoon salt	rinsed and drained
1 beaten egg white	1 15-ounce can tomato sauce
¹⁄₄ cup fat-free milk	1 4-ounce can diced green chile
2 tablespoons cooking oil	peppers, drained
³⁄₄ cup water	2 teaspoons chili powder
1 cup chopped onion	1 tablespoon cold water
1 clove garlic, minced	1¹⁄₂ teaspoons cornstarch
	Shredded cheddar cheese (optional)

1

In a medium bowl stir together flour, cornmeal, baking powder, and salt; set aside. In a small bowl combine egg white, milk, and oil; set aside.

2

In a 10-inch skillet combine the ³⁄₄ cup water, the onion, and garlic. Bring to boiling; reduce heat. Cover and simmer about 5 minutes or until tender. Stir in chickpeas, kidney beans, tomato sauce, green chile peppers, and chili powder.

3

In a small bowl stir the 1 tablespoon cold water into the cornstarch. Stir into bean mixture. Cook and stir until slightly thickened and bubbly. Reduce heat.

4

For dumplings, add milk mixture to cornmeal mixture; stir just until combined. Drop dumpling batter from a tablespoon to make 5 mounds on top of the hot bean mixture.

5

Cover and simmer for 10 to 12 minutes or until a toothpick inserted into the center of a dumpling comes out clean.

6

To serve, ladle chili into bowls. If desired, top with shredded cheese.

Nutrition Facts per serving: 306 calories, 8 g total fat, 0 mg cholesterol, 685 mg sodium, 51 g carbohydrate, 13 g protein.

MAIN-DISH SALADS

For a refreshing yet filling meal, you won't go wrong with one of these vegetable, pasta, bean, or grain combos.

Tortellini-Vegetable Salad
(see recipe, page 180)

TORTELLINI-VEGETABLE SALAD

This irresistible pasta and greens salad will go a long way toward curing those dinnertime hunger pangs. (Pictured on page 179.)

Start to Finish: 20 minutes **Makes:** 4 servings

1 9-ounce package refrigerated cheese-filled tortellini
6 cups torn mixed salad greens
1½ cups sliced fresh mushrooms
1 medium red sweet pepper, cut into thin bite-size strips
¼ cup snipped fresh basil
¼ cup white wine vinegar or white vinegar

2 tablespoons water
2 tablespoons olive oil
2 teaspoons sugar
2 cloves garlic, minced
¼ teaspoon ground black pepper
½ cup fat-free toasted garlic-and-onion croutons

1
Cook tortellini according to package directions, except omit any oil or salt. Drain tortellini. Rinse with cold water; drain again.

2
In a large bowl combine tortellini, salad greens, mushrooms, sweet pepper, and basil.

3
For dressing, in a screw-top jar combine vinegar, the water, oil, sugar, garlic, and black pepper. Cover and shake well. Pour over tortellini mixture; toss to coat.

4
To serve, divide tortellini mixture among 4 dinner plates. Pass the croutons.

Nutrition Facts per serving: 302 calories, 12 g total fat, 30 mg cholesterol, 288 mg sodium, 40 g carbohydrate, 12 g protein.

FRIED TOFU AND WATERCRESS SALAD

A melange of vinaigrette-dressed greens and crisp tofu triangles put this delectable salad in a league of its own.

Start to Finish: 30 minutes **Makes:** 4 servings

12 ounces extra-firm light tofu (fresh bean curd), drained

3 tablespoons tamari sauce or reduced-sodium soy sauce

1/3 cup rice vinegar

2 tablespoons grated fresh ginger

1 tablespoon sugar

1 teaspoon Dijon-style mustard or 1/4 teaspoon dry mustard

1/4 teaspoon salt

1/3 cup salad oil

1/3 cup cornmeal

1 tablespoon sesame seeds, toasted

2 teaspoons cooking oil

6 cups torn fresh spinach

1 bunch watercress (about 1 1/2 cups), stems removed

1 cup sliced fresh mushrooms

1 cup cherry tomatoes

1 medium red onion, halved lengthwise and thinly sliced

Sesame seeds, toasted

1

Cut tofu crosswise into eight 1/2-inch slices. In a 2-quart rectangular baking dish arrange slices in a single layer. Pour tamari sauce or soy sauce over tofu; turn slices to coat. Let stand for 15 minutes.

2

Meanwhile, for vinaigrette, in a blender container or food processor bowl combine vinegar, ginger, sugar, mustard, and salt. Cover and blend or process until combined. With blender or processor running, add the 1/3 cup oil in a thin, steady stream. Blend or process for 15 seconds more. Set aside.

3

Drain tofu, discarding tamari sauce or soy sauce. In a shallow dish combine cornmeal and the 1 tablespoon sesame seeds. Carefully dip tofu slices in cornmeal mixture to lightly coat both sides. In a large nonstick skillet cook tofu in the 2 teaspoons hot oil for 5 to 6 minutes or until crisp and hot, carefully turning once. (You may need to cook tofu in 2 batches; do not crowd skillet.)

4

In an extra-large bowl combine spinach, watercress, mushrooms, cherry tomatoes, and red onion. Pour the vinaigrette over spinach mixture; toss to coat.

5

To serve, divide spinach mixture among 4 dinner plates. Cut each tofu slice in half diagonally. Arrange the tofu over spinach mixture. If desired, sprinkle with additional sesame seeds.

Nutrition Facts per serving: 330 calories, 23 g total fat, 0 mg cholesterol, 1,030 mg sodium, 21 g carbohydrate, 11 g protein.

FONTINA AND MELON SALAD

Serve this refreshing salad with your favorite fruit muffins.

Start to Finish: 25 minutes **Makes:** 4 servings

1½ cups dried large bow ties (farfalle)
(6 ounces)
2 cups cantaloupe and/or honeydew
melon chunks
1 cup cubed fontina or Swiss cheese
(4 ounces)

⅓ cup bottled fat-free poppy seed
salad dressing
1 to 2 tablespoons snipped fresh mint
2 cups watercress, stems removed
2 cantaloupe, halved and seeded
(optional)

1
Cook pasta according to package directions. Drain. Rinse with cold water; drain again.

2
In a large bowl toss together pasta, cantaloupe or honeydew melon chunks, and cheese. In a small bowl combine salad dressing and mint; pour over pasta mixture, tossing gently to coat. If desired, cover and chill in the refrigerator for up to 24 hours.

3
To serve, stir watercress into pasta mixture. If desired, serve salad in cantaloupe halves.

Nutrition Facts per serving: 319 calories, 11 g total fat, 73 mg cholesterol, 309 mg sodium, 41 g carbohydrate, 14 g protein.

GRAPEFRUIT AND BLACK BEAN SALAD

Pass some whole wheat tortillas to go with this citrusy main-dish salad. If you like, substitute Monterey Jack cheese with jalapeño peppers for the regular Monterey Jack.

Start to Finish: 20 minutes **Makes:** 4 servings

6 cups torn mixed salad greens

2 medium red grapefruit, peeled and thinly sliced

1 15-ounce can black beans, rinsed and drained

1 medium cucumber, halved lengthwise and sliced

¾ cup shredded carrots

2 ounces Monterey Jack cheese, cubed

¼ cup frozen grapefruit juice concentrate, thawed

2 teaspoons honey

2 teaspoons salad oil

2 teaspoons water

⅛ teaspoon salt

⅛ teaspoon ground cumin

1

Line a serving platter with the greens. Arrange grapefruit slices on top of greens. In a medium bowl combine beans, cucumber, and carrots. Spoon mixture over grapefruit. Top with cheese.

2

For dressing, in a screw-top jar combine grapefruit juice concentrate, honey, oil, the water, salt, and cumin. Cover and shake well.

3

To serve, drizzle some of the dressing over salad. Pass remaining dressing.

Nutrition Facts per serving: 239 calories, 7 g total fat, 13 mg cholesterol, 422 mg sodium, 37 g carbohydrate, 13 g protein.

TOFU-DRESSED VEGETARIAN SALAD

If blue cheese isn't on your list of favorite cheeses, try feta or goat cheese instead.

Start to Finish: 25 minutes **Makes:** 4 servings

½ cup mayonnaise or salad dressing
4 ounces tofu (fresh bean curd)
½ teaspoon fines herbes, crushed
1 to 2 tablespoons milk (optional)
5 cups torn romaine
1 cup shredded radicchio
1 cup enoki mushrooms or sliced
  button mushrooms

1 medium yellow or green sweet
  pepper, cut into bite-size pieces*
4 ounces blue cheese, crumbled
  (1 cup)
½ cup broken pecans, toasted
¼ cup sliced green onions

1

For dressing, in a food processor bowl or blender container combine the mayonnaise or salad dressing, tofu, and fines herbes. Cover and process or blend until smooth. If necessary, stir in enough of the milk to make desired consistency.

2

To serve, arrange the romaine, radicchio, mushrooms, sweet pepper, cheese, pecans, and green onions on 4 dinner plates. Serve with dressing.

Nutrition Facts per serving: 509 calories, 48 g total fat, 43 mg cholesterol, 617 mg sodium, 11 g carbohydrate, 12 g protein.

*Note: For fancy pepper shapes, use a star, moon, heart, or other shape of hors d'oeuvres cutter to cut the sweet pepper.

DELI-STYLE PASTA SALAD

Ideal for everything from a quick supper to a block party feast, this tortellini and veggie salad goes together in just minutes.

Start to Finish: 25 minutes **Makes:** 4 servings

½ of a 16-ounce package
    (about 2 cups) frozen
    cheese-filled tortellini or one
    9-ounce package refrigerated
    cheese-filled tortellini
1½ cups broccoli florets
1 large carrot, thinly sliced
¼ cup white wine vinegar
2 tablespoons olive oil

1 teaspoon dried Italian seasoning,
    crushed
1 teaspoon Dijon-style mustard
¼ teaspoon ground black pepper
⅛ teaspoon garlic powder
1 medium red or yellow sweet pepper,
    cut into thin, bite-size strips
Fresh chives with blossoms
    (optional)

1

In a large saucepan cook tortellini according to package directions, except omit any oil or salt and add broccoli and carrot for the last 3 minutes of cooking. Drain tortellini and vegetables. Rinse with cold water; drain again.

2

Meanwhile, for dressing, in a screw-top jar combine the vinegar, oil, Italian seasoning, mustard, black pepper, and garlic powder. Cover and shake well. Set aside.

3

In a large bowl combine the tortellini mixture and sweet pepper. Shake dressing. Pour over tortellini mixture; toss gently to coat.

4

To serve, divide among 4 dinner plates. If desired, garnish with fresh chives.

Nutrition Facts per serving: 305 calories, 12 g total fat, 30 mg cholesterol, 315 mg sodium, 41 g carbohydrate, 13 g protein.

THE NEW CHEF'S SALAD

This unique bean and cheese salad is a meatless version of the American classic that typically features greens with meats and cheeses on top.

Start to Finish: 25 minutes **Makes:** 4 servings

$^1/_3$ cup fat-free mayonnaise dressing or salad dressing

$^1/_3$ cup light dairy sour cream

2 teaspoons white wine vinegar

2 cloves garlic, minced

$1^1/_2$ teaspoons snipped fresh marjoram or $^1/_2$ teaspoon dried marjoram, crushed

$^1/_4$ teaspoon dry mustard

$^1/_8$ teaspoon salt

3 tablespoons fat-free milk

2 cups Boston or Bibb lettuce

2 cups torn fresh spinach

1 cup shredded red cabbage

1 15-ounce can reduced-sodium red kidney beans or chickpeas (garbanzo beans), rinsed and drained

1 cup shredded reduced-fat cheddar cheese (4 ounces)

1 small zucchini, thinly sliced

1 small green or red sweet pepper, thinly sliced

$^1/_2$ cup halved cherry tomatoes

$^1/_2$ cup thinly sliced radishes

1 hard-cooked egg, sliced

Paprika (optional)

1

For dressing, in a small bowl combine mayonnaise dressing or salad dressing, sour cream, vinegar, garlic, marjoram, mustard, and salt. Stir in the milk.

2

In a large bowl toss together the lettuce, spinach, red cabbage, kidney beans or chickpeas, cheese, zucchini, sweet pepper, tomatoes, and radishes. Pour the dressing over all; toss to coat.

3

To serve, divide mixture among 4 dinner plates. Arrange egg slices on salad. If desired, sprinkle with paprika.

Nutrition Facts per serving: 275 calories, 8 g total fat, 76 mg cholesterol, 740 mg sodium, 34 g carbohydrate, 20 g protein.

GRILLED VEGETABLE SALAD WITH GARLIC DRESSING

To save last-minute fuss, grill the vegetables ahead and chill them in the refrigerator.

Start to Finish: 30 minutes **Makes:** 4 servings

4 or 5 yellow sunburst or pattypan squash

2 red and/or yellow sweet peppers

2 Japanese eggplants, halved lengthwise

1 medium zucchini or yellow summer squash, halved lengthwise

1 tablespoon olive oil

2 cups dried tortiglioni or rigatoni (about 5 ounces)

1 recipe Roasted Garlic Dressing

3/4 cup cubed fontina cheese (3 ounces)

1 to 2 tablespoons snipped fresh flat-leaf parsley or regular parsley

Fresh flat-leaf parsley sprigs

1

In a covered medium saucepan cook sunburst or pattypan squash in a small amount of boiling water for 3 minutes; drain. Halve sweet peppers lengthwise; remove and discard stems, seeds, and membranes. Brush sunburst or pattypan squash, sweet peppers, eggplants, and zucchini or yellow summer squash with oil. Grill vegetables on grill rack of an uncovered grill directly over medium-hot coals for 8 to 12 minutes or until vegetables are tender, turning occasionally. Remove vegetables from grill; cool slightly. Cut vegetables into 1-inch pieces.

2

Meanwhile, cook pasta according to package directions. Drain. Rinse with cold water; drain again.

3

In a large bowl combine pasta and grilled vegetables. Pour Roasted Garlic Dressing over salad. Toss lightly to coat. Stir in cheese; sprinkle with snipped parsley. If desired, garnish with parsley sprigs.

Roasted Garlic Dressing: In a screw-top jar combine 3 tablespoons balsamic vinegar or red wine vinegar, 2 tablespoons olive oil, 1 tablespoon water, 1 teaspoon bottled roasted minced garlic, 1/4 teaspoon salt, and 1/4 teaspoon ground black pepper. Cover and shake well.

Nutrition Facts per serving: 369 calories, 19 g total fat, 61 mg cholesterol, 317 mg sodium, 40 g carbohydrate, 12 g protein.

TARRAGON BEAN SALAD

Fresh tarragon and Dijon-style mustard add zip to this vibrant tomato-and-bean match-up.

Start to Finish: 20 minutes **Makes:** 5 servings

1 15-ounce can red kidney beans,
  rinsed and drained
1 15-ounce can butter beans, rinsed
  and drained
1 15-ounce can chickpeas (garbanzo
  beans), rinsed and drained
1½ cups chopped seeded tomatoes or
  halved cherry or grape tomatoes
1 medium carrot, cut into thin
  bite-size strips
2 tablespoons finely chopped red onion

3 tablespoons olive oil
2 tablespoons red wine vinegar
2 tablespoons Dijon-style mustard
1 tablespoon snipped fresh tarragon
  or ½ teaspoon dried tarragon,
  crushed
1 teaspoon sugar
¼ teaspoon salt
⅛ teaspoon ground black pepper
  Lettuce leaves

1

In a large bowl combine the kidney beans, butter beans, chickpeas, tomatoes, carrot strips, and red onion. Set aside.

2

For dressing, in a screw-top jar combine oil, vinegar, mustard, tarragon, sugar, salt, and black pepper. Cover and shake well.

3

Pour the dressing over bean mixture; toss gently to coat. Line 4 dinner plates with lettuce. Divide bean mixture among lettuce-lined plates.

Nutrition Facts per serving: 334 calories, 10 g total fat, 0 mg cholesterol, 1005 mg sodium, 49 g carbohydrate, 14 g protein.

TACO SALAD

The leftover black beans are no problem. Stir them into your next batch of chili or vegetable soup. Or, mix them with some salsa for a healthful baked potato topper.

Start to Finish: 20 minutes **Makes:** 4 servings

1 15-ounce can navy or Great Northern beans, rinsed and drained
$^1/_2$ of a 15-ounce can reduced-sodium black beans, rinsed and drained
$^3/_4$ cup salsa
1 teaspoon chili powder
$^1/_2$ teaspoon garlic powder
6 cups shredded iceberg or leaf lettuce

2 medium tomatoes, chopped
1 cup chopped green sweet pepper
$^1/_4$ cup shredded reduced-fat cheddar cheese (1 ounce)
$^1/_4$ cup sliced pitted ripe olives (optional)
1 cup baked tortilla chips
Fat-free dairy sour cream (optional)

1

In a medium saucepan stir together the navy or Great Northern beans, black beans, salsa, chili powder, and garlic powder. Cook, uncovered, over medium heat until heated through, stirring occasionally.

2

Meanwhile, divide the shredded lettuce among 4 dinner plates. Top with bean mixture, tomatoes, sweet pepper, cheese, and, if desired, olives. Serve with tortilla chips and, if desired, sour cream.

Nutrition Facts per serving: 264 calories, 3 g total fat, 5 mg cholesterol, 797 mg sodium, 43 g carbohydrate, 15 g protein.

MIDDLE EASTERN BULGUR-SPINACH SALAD

Bulgur or cracked wheat finds its way into numerous Middle Eastern dishes. Here it costars with spinach, chickpeas, onion, and apple.

Start to Finish: 30 minutes **Makes:** 4 servings

1 cup bulgur
1 cup boiling water
$\frac{1}{2}$ cup plain yogurt
$\frac{1}{4}$ cup bottled red wine vinaigrette
    salad dressing
2 tablespoons snipped fresh parsley
$\frac{1}{2}$ teaspoon ground cumin

6 cups torn fresh spinach
1 15-ounce can chickpeas (garbanzo
    beans), rinsed and drained
1 cup coarsely chopped apple
$\frac{1}{2}$ of a medium red onion, thinly sliced
    and separated into rings
3 tablespoons raisins (optional)

1

In a medium bowl combine bulgur and the boiling water. Let stand about 20 minutes (bulgur should have absorbed all of the water).

2

Meanwhile, for dressing, in a small bowl stir together yogurt, salad dressing, parsley, and cumin.

3

To serve, in a large bowl combine bulgur, spinach, chickpeas, apple, onion, and, if desired, raisins. Pour dressing over salad. Toss lightly to coat. Divide among 4 salad bowls or dinner plates.

Nutrition Facts per serving: 340 calories, 11 g total fat, 2 mg cholesterol, 673 mg sodium, 53 g carbohydrate, 13 g protein.

PENNE SALAD WITH ITALIAN BEANS AND GORGONZOLA

If you like, substitute a 9-ounce package frozen Italian green beans for the fresh beans. Just thaw them and cook them with the pasta for 3 to 4 minutes.

Start to Finish: 25 minutes **Makes:** 4 servings

6 ounces dried penne (mostaccioli), cut ziti, or elbow macaroni

8 ounces fresh Italian green beans, trimmed and bias-sliced into 1- to 2-inch pieces

1/3 cup bottled fat-free Italian salad dressing

1 tablespoon snipped fresh tarragon or 1/2 teaspoon dried tarragon, crushed

1/2 teaspoon freshly ground black pepper

2 cups torn radicchio or 1 cup finely shredded red cabbage

4 cups fresh sorrel or spinach leaves

1/2 cup crumbled Gorgonzola or other blue cheese (2 ounces)

1

Cook pasta according to package directions, adding green beans for the last 5 to 7 minutes of cooking. Drain pasta and beans. Rinse pasta and beans with cold water; drain again.

2

In a large bowl combine Italian salad dressing, tarragon, and pepper. Add pasta mixture and radicchio or cabbage; toss gently to coat.

3

To serve, divide sorrel or spinach leaves among 4 salad bowls or dinner plates. Top with pasta mixture. Sprinkle with cheese.

Nutrition Facts per serving: 269 calories, 6 g total fat, 13 mg cholesterol, 566 mg sodium, 42 g carbohydrate, 12 g protein.

MEXICAN FIESTA SALAD

When corn on the cob is in season, use ¹/₂ cup fresh corn kernels in this spunky salad, and save a few of the cornhusks to line the serving bowl.

Start to Finish: 30 minutes **Makes:** 4 servings

2 cups dried penne (mostaccioli) or
  corkscrew macaroni (rotini)
  (about 6 ounces)
¹/₂ cup frozen whole kernel corn
¹/₂ cup light dairy sour cream
¹/₃ cup mild or medium bottled chunky
  salsa
1 tablespoon snipped fresh cilantro

1 tablespoon lime juice
1 15-ounce can black beans, rinsed
  and drained
3 medium plum tomatoes, chopped
1 medium zucchini, chopped
¹/₂ cup shredded sharp cheddar cheese
  (2 ounces)
Fresh cilantro sprigs (optional)

1

Cook pasta according to package directions, adding the corn for the last 5 minutes of cooking. Drain pasta and corn. Rinse with cold water; drain again.

2

Meanwhile, for dressing, in a small bowl stir together sour cream, salsa, snipped cilantro, and lime juice. Set dressing aside.

3

In a large bowl combine pasta-corn mixture, black beans, tomatoes, and zucchini. Set aside a little of the cheese for topping; add remaining cheese to pasta mixture. Pour dressing over pasta mixture. Toss lightly to coat. (If desired, cover and chill in the refrigerator for up to 24 hours. Before serving, if necessary, stir in enough milk to moisten.) Top with reserved cheese. If desired, garnish with cilantro sprigs.

Nutrition Facts per serving: 373 calories, 9 g total fat, 19 mg cholesterol, 470 mg sodium, 61 g carbohydrate, 20 g protein.

PASTA-FRUIT SALAD

Fruit, pasta, cheddar cheese, and nuts add up to a refreshing protein-packed main dish.

Start to Finish: 30 minutes **Makes:** 4 servings

- 4 ounces dried radiatore, medium shell macaroni, or rotini
- 1 16-ounce can apricot halves in light syrup or one 16-ounce can peach slices in light syrup, drained
- 1 8-ounce can pineapple tidbits (juice packed) or one 11-ounce can mandarin orange sections, drained
- 1 cup seedless red or green grapes, halved
- $^3/_4$ cup shredded cheddar cheese (3 ounces)
- $^1/_4$ cup broken pecans or walnuts
- $^1/_2$ of an 8-ounce container vanilla yogurt
- 1 tablespoon frozen orange juice concentrate
- $^1/_8$ teaspoon ground nutmeg
  Lettuce leaves

1

Cook pasta according to package directions. Drain. Rinse pasta with cold water; drain again.

2

Meanwhile, cut up apricot halves or peach slices. In a large bowl toss together apricots or peaches, pineapple tidbits or orange sections, grapes, cheese, and nuts. Add pasta. Toss to mix. Place in freezer until serving time (up to 30 minutes).

3

For dressing, stir together yogurt, orange juice concentrate, and nutmeg. Add the dressing to pasta mixture; toss to coat. Line 4 salad plates with lettuce leaves. Divide the pasta mixture among lettuce-lined plates.

Nutrition Facts per serving: 411 calories, 13 g total fat, 24 mg cholesterol, 163 mg sodium, 65 g carbohydrate, 12 g protein.

SANDWICHES & PIZZAS

*Easy, eye-catching, and extra good, these mealtime
headliners make feeding the family a pleasure.*

Eggplant Panini
(see recipe, page 208)

GARDEN VEGGIE BURGERS

Dress up store-bought meatless burger patties with grilled onion and a wilted spinach and feta cheese topper.

Prep: 10 minutes **Grill:** 15 minutes **Makes:** 4 servings

$1/4$ cup bottled vinaigrette salad dressing

2 medium red onions, cut into $1/2$-inch slices

4 refrigerated or frozen meatless burger patties

4 cups fresh spinach leaves

1 clove garlic, minced

1 tablespoon olive oil

$1/2$ cup crumbled feta cheese (2 ounces)

4 hamburger buns, split

1

Let salad dressing stand at room temperature while grilling onions and patties. Grill onions on the rack of an uncovered grill directly over medium coals for 15 to 20 minutes or until tender, turning once halfway through grilling. Grill patties alongside the onions for 8 to 10 minutes or until heated through, turning once halfway through grilling. Brush grilled onions with the salad dressing.

2

Meanwhile, for spinach topping, in a large skillet cook and stir the spinach and garlic in hot oil over medium-high heat about 30 seconds or just until spinach is wilted. Remove from heat. Stir in feta cheese.

3

To serve, place grilled onion slices on bottom of buns. Top with grilled burger patties, spinach topping, and bun tops.

Nutrition Facts per serving: 350 calories, 14 g total fat, 17 mg cholesterol, 920 mg sodium, 37 g carbohydrate, 21 g protein.

EGGPLANT PANINI

This sandwich is Italian all the way from its name right on through to old-country ingredients, such as arugula, Romano cheese, and focaccia. (Pictured on page 205.)

Start to Finish: 25 minutes **Makes:** 6 servings

1 cup torn arugula
2 teaspoons red wine vinegar
1 teaspoon olive oil
1/3 cup seasoned fine dry bread crumbs
2 tablespoons grated Romano or
    Parmesan cheese
1 egg
1 tablespoon milk
2 tablespoons all-purpose flour
1/2 teaspoon salt

1 medium eggplant, cut crosswise into
    1/2-inch slices
1 tablespoon olive oil
3 ounces fresh mozzarella cheese,
    thinly sliced
1 12-inch plain or seasoned Italian
    flatbread (focaccia), halved
    horizontally*
1 large tomato, thinly sliced

1

In a small bowl toss together the arugula, vinegar, and the 1 teaspoon oil; set aside. In a shallow dish stir together the bread crumbs and Romano or Parmesan cheese. In another shallow dish beat together the egg and milk. In a third shallow dish stir together the flour and salt. Dip the eggplant slices into flour mixture to coat. Dip the slices into egg mixture, then coat both sides with crumb mixture.

2

In a 12-inch nonstick skillet cook eggplant slices in the 1 tablespoon hot oil over medium heat for 6 to 8 minutes or until lightly browned, turning to brown evenly. (Add more oil as necessary during cooking.) Top the eggplant with mozzarella cheese; reduce heat to low. Cover and cook just until cheese begins to melt.

3

To serve, place the eggplant slices, cheese sides up, on bottom half of bread. Top with the arugula mixture, tomato slices, and top half of bread. To serve, cut into wedges or slices.

Nutrition Facts per serving: 318 calories, 10 g total fat, 48 mg cholesterol, 447 mg sodium, 45 g carbohydrate, 13 g protein.

*Note: For easier slicing, purchase focaccia that is at least 2 1/2 inches thick.

SAUTÉED ONION AND TOMATO SANDWICHES

If you like, substitute sweet Vidalia or Walla Walla onions or red onions for the regular onions in this colorful sandwich.

Start to Finish: 20 minutes **Makes:** 4 servings

- 2 medium onions, sliced
- 1 teaspoon olive oil
- 8 slices hearty whole grain bread
  Honey mustard
- 3 small tomatoes, thinly sliced

- 4 lettuce leaves, shredded (optional)
  Small fresh basil leaves
- 4 ounces spreadable Brie cheese or
  soft-style cream cheese

1

In a large skillet cook onion slices in hot oil over medium-high heat for 5 to 7 minutes or until tender and just starting to brown. Remove from heat; cool onions slightly. Meanwhile, if desired, toast bread.

2

To assemble, lightly spread 1 side of each of 4 bread slices with honey mustard. Top with onion slices, tomato slices, lettuce, if desired, and basil. Spread 1 side of each of the remaining bread slices with Brie cheese; place on top of sandwiches, cheese sides down.

Nutrition Facts per serving: 287 calories, 12 g total fat, 28 mg cholesterol, 490 mg sodium, 35 g carbohydrate, 12 g protein.

FALAFEL BURGERS IN PITAS

Traditional falafel are deep-fried croquettes made from ground chickpeas. In this recipe, the falafel is shaped into a burger and pan fried to save calories and fat.

Start to Finish: 30 minutes **Makes:** 4 servings

¼ cup fine dry bread crumbs	Milk
1 15-ounce can chickpeas (garbanzo beans), rinsed and drained	1 tablespoon olive oil
	2 large pita bread rounds, halved crosswise
½ cup chopped onion	½ of a small cucumber, thinly sliced
2 cloves garlic, minced	1 small tomato, thinly sliced
1 teaspoon ground cumin	¼ cup bottled cucumber ranch or creamy cucumber salad dressing
¼ cup snipped fresh parsley	
2 tablespoons all-purpose flour	

1
Place the bread crumbs in a shallow dish; set aside. In a food processor bowl combine the chickpeas, onion, garlic, and cumin. Cover and process until mixture is coarsely ground. Stir in the parsley and flour.

2
Shape the chickpea mixture into 4 patties, each 3 inches in diameter. Carefully brush patties with milk, then coat both sides with bread crumbs.

3
In a large nonstick skillet cook patties in hot oil over medium heat for 8 to 10 minutes or until patties are lightly browned, turning to brown evenly. (Add more oil as necessary during cooking.)

4
To serve, fill the pita halves with the patties, cucumber, and tomato slices. Drizzle with salad dressing.

Nutrition Facts per serving: 337 calories, 13 g total fat, 0 mg cholesterol, 746 mg sodium, 45 g carbohydrate, 10 g protein.

ARTICHOKE AND BASIL HERO

A basil and caper sauce packs a powerful punch in this all-vegetable sandwich.

Start to Finish: 25 minutes   **Makes:** 6 servings

1 cup firmly packed fresh basil leaves

¼ cup olive oil or salad oil

2 tablespoons grated Parmesan cheese

1 tablespoon capers, drained

1 tablespoon white wine vinegar

2 teaspoons Dijon-style mustard

1 clove garlic, quartered

1 16-ounce loaf French bread

1 14-ounce can artichoke hearts, drained and sliced

4 ounces provolone cheese, sliced

1 medium tomato, thinly sliced

2 cups torn fresh spinach

1

In a blender container or food processor bowl combine the basil, oil, Parmesan cheese, capers, vinegar, mustard, and garlic. Cover; blend or process until nearly smooth. Set aside.

2

Cut bread in half lengthwise. Hollow out each half, leaving a ½- to 1-inch shell. (Reserve bread crumbs for another use.) Spread the basil mixture over the cut side of each bread half. On the bottom half, layer artichoke hearts, cheese, tomato, and spinach. Cover with bread top.

3

To serve, cut sandwich crosswise into 6 pieces.

Nutrition Facts per serving: 396 calories, 17 g total fat, 14 mg cholesterol, 887 mg sodium, 46 g carbohydrate, 15 g protein.

CHEESY EGGPLANT-PEPPER CALZONE

For a quick salad to go along with this hearty fold-over sandwich, drain a jar of marinated artichoke hearts. Toss the artichokes with ripe olives and serve the mixture on lettuce leaves.

Prep: 20 minutes **Bake:** 12 minutes **Makes:** 4 servings

1 small eggplant,* peeled and cut into ½-inch cubes (4 cups)
1 teaspoon bottled minced garlic or 2 cloves garlic, minced
2 tablespoons cooking oil or olive oil
½ of a small red sweet pepper,* cut into thin, bite-size strips
½ teaspoon dried Italian seasoning, crushed
½ teaspoon salt

¼ teaspoon ground black pepper
1 10-ounce package refrigerated pizza dough
2 cups shredded Italian-blend cheeses (mozzarella and provolone) or shredded mozzarella cheese (8 ounces)
Milk
Grated Parmesan cheese

1

In a large skillet cook the eggplant and garlic in hot oil about 5 minutes or until tender. Stir in sweet pepper, Italian seasoning, salt, and black pepper. Cook and stir just until sweet pepper is tender. Remove from heat.

2

Unroll pizza dough on an ungreased baking sheet, forming a rectangle. Spread vegetable mixture on half of the dough rectangle, coming to within 1 inch of edges and stopping at middle of rectangle. Sprinkle shredded cheese over vegetables. Moisten edges with water; fold side of dough with no filling over filling and seal edges with tines of a fork. Prick top with a fork. Brush with milk; sprinkle with Parmesan cheese.

3

Bake in a 425°F oven for 12 to 15 minutes or until golden.

4

To serve, cut into wedges.

Nutrition Facts per serving: 419 calories, 22 g total fat, 37 mg cholesterol, 906 mg sodium, 35 g carbohydrate, 20 g protein.

*Note: For an even faster option, use 2 cups leftover cooked vegetables in place of the eggplant and sweet pepper. Omit the oil, salt, and pepper. Sprinkle the Italian seasoning over the vegetables along with the shredded cheese.

COUSCOUS BURRITOS

Couscous adds a Moroccan touch to this Tex-Mex wrap-and-roll tempter.

Start to Finish: 20 minutes **Makes:** 4 servings

8 8-inch flavored or plain flour
   tortillas
1 cup vegetable broth
1 4-ounce can diced green chile
   peppers, drained
1/4 teaspoon ground turmeric
   Dash ground black pepper

2/3 cup quick-cooking couscous
1/4 cup sliced green onions
1 cup chopped tomatoes
3/4 cup chopped green sweet pepper
1/2 cup finely shredded Mexican-blend
   cheeses (2 ounces)
   Bottled salsa (optional)

1

Wrap the tortillas in foil. Heat in a 350°F oven for 10 minutes to soften.(Or wrap tortillas in microwave-safe paper towels. Microwave on 100-percent [high] power for 30 seconds.)

2

Meanwhile, in a small saucepan combine the broth, green chile peppers, turmeric, and black pepper. Bring to boiling. Remove from heat. Stir in couscous and green onions. Cover and let stand for 5 minutes. Fluff couscous with a fork. Stir in tomatoes and sweet pepper.

3

To assemble each burrito, spoon about 1/3 cup of the couscous mixture onto a tortilla. Top with 1 tablespoon of the cheese. Roll up the tortilla. If desired, serve with salsa.

Nutrition Facts per serving: 380 calories, 10 g total fat, 13 mg cholesterol, 679 mg sodium, 59 g carbohydrate, 13 g protein.

MU SHU VEGETABLE ROLL-UPS

Flour tortillas substitute for the traditional thin pancakes in this adaptation of an Asian favorite. Brighten each serving with a cherry tomato flower and a green onion brush.

Start to Finish: 35 minutes **Makes:** 4 or 5 servings

2 tablespoons water
2 tablespoons soy sauce
$^1/_2$ teaspoon sugar
$^1/_2$ teaspoon cornstarch
8 to 10 8-inch flour tortillas
1 tablespoon cooking oil
1 teaspoon grated fresh ginger
2 cloves garlic, minced
2 medium carrots, cut into thin, bite-size strips
$^1/_2$ of a small head cabbage, shredded

1 medium zucchini, cut into thin, bite-size strips
4 ounces fresh mushrooms, sliced
$^1/_2$ of a medium jicama, peeled and cut into thin, bite-size strips
8 ounces firm tofu (fresh bean curd), well drained and cut into $^3/_4$-inch cubes
8 green onions, sliced
$^1/_4$ cup hoisin sauce

1

For sauce, in a small bowl stir together the water, soy sauce, sugar, and cornstarch. Set aside. Stack tortillas; wrap in foil. Heat in a 350°F oven for 10 minutes to soften. (Or place tortillas, half at a time, between layers of microwave-safe paper towels. Microwave on 100-percent [high] power for $1^1/_2$ to 2 minutes or until warm.)

2

Meanwhile, pour oil into a wok or large skillet. (Add more oil as necessary during cooking.) Heat over medium-high heat. Stir-fry ginger and garlic in hot oil for 15 seconds. Add carrots; stir-fry for 1 minute. Add cabbage and zucchini; stir-fry for 1 minute more. Add mushrooms and jicama; stir-fry for 1 to 2 minutes more or until vegetables are crisp-tender. Push vegetables from the center of the wok.

3

Stir sauce. Add sauce to the center of the wok. Cook and stir until thickened and bubbly. Add tofu and sliced green onions. Gently stir all ingredients together to coat with sauce. Cover and cook about 2 minutes more or until heated through.

4

Spread warm tortillas with hoisin sauce. Spoon vegetable mixture onto tortillas. Fold over 1 side of each tortilla to cover some of the filling. Fold the 2 adjacent sides of each tortilla over filling. If necessary, secure with toothpicks. Serve immediately.

Nutrition Facts per serving: 377 calories, 11 g total fat, 0 mg cholesterol, 1,048 mg sodium, 55 g carbohydrate, 14 g protein.

BLACK BEAN-VEGETABLE BURRITOS

*Simmering the bean mixture while the tortillas heat in the oven
means dinner will be ready in just minutes.*

Start to Finish: 20 minutes **Makes:** 4 servings

8 7- or 8-inch fat-free flour tortillas
1 medium onion, chopped
½ of a medium green or red sweet
    pepper, cut into thin strips
1 tablespoon lime juice
¼ teaspoon bottled minced garlic
2 teaspoons olive oil
1 15-ounce can black beans, rinsed
    and drained

½ cup loose-pack frozen whole kernel
    corn
¼ teaspoon ground cumin
¼ teaspoon chili powder
⅛ teaspoon ground black pepper
1 cup shredded reduced-fat Monterey
    Jack cheese (4 ounces)
    Light dairy sour cream (optional)
    Bottled salsa (optional)

1

Stack tortillas and wrap tightly in foil. Heat in a 350°F oven for 10 minutes to soften. Set aside and keep warm.

2

Meanwhile, in a medium saucepan cook onion, sweet pepper, lime juice, and garlic in hot oil for 3 to 5 minutes or until vegetables are tender. Stir in black beans, corn, cumin, chili powder, and black pepper. Cook over medium heat for 4 to 5 minutes or until corn is tender and mixture is heated through.

3

To assemble each burrito, spoon about ⅓ cup of the bean mixture onto a tortilla just below center. Top with 2 tablespoons of the cheese. Fold 1 edge of tortilla over filling. Fold filled tortilla in half. If desired, serve with sour cream and salsa.

Nutrition Facts per serving: 420 calories, 8 g total fat, 20 mg cholesterol, 1,128 mg sodium, 70 g carbohydrate, 20 g protein.

CHICKPEA PITA POCKETS

Poppy seed dressing and Swiss cheese are enticing additions to this fruit and chickpea sandwich.

Start to Finish: 20 minutes **Makes:** 4 servings

1 15-ounce can chickpeas (garbanzo beans), rinsed and drained
1 cup shredded fresh spinach or lettuce
$^2/_3$ cup seedless grapes, halved
$^1/_2$ cup finely chopped red sweet pepper
$^1/_3$ cup thinly sliced celery

$^1/_4$ cup finely chopped onion
$^1/_4$ cup mayonnaise or salad dressing
2 tablespoons bottled poppy seed salad dressing or desired creamy salad dressing
4 pita bread rounds, halved crosswise
$^1/_2$ cup finely shredded Swiss cheese (2 ounces)

1

In a large bowl combine chickpeas, spinach or lettuce, grapes, red sweet pepper, celery, and onion.

2

In a small bowl stir together mayonnaise or salad dressing and poppy seed salad dressing or desired creamy salad dressing. Add to chickpea mixture, stirring until combined.

3

To serve, spoon chickpea mixture into pita bread halves. Top with cheese.

Nutrition Facts per serving: 476 calories, 21 g total fat, 21 mg cholesterol, 857 mg sodium, 58 g carbohydrate, 15 g protein.

CHEESE AND VEGGIE SANDWICHES

Tomato soup is the ideal serve-along for this cottage cheese-and-veggie medley.

Start to Finish: 15 minutes **Makes:** 4 servings

1½ cups cottage cheese, drained
¼ cup shredded carrot
¼ cup chopped green sweet pepper or celery
½ teaspoon finely snipped chives

¼ cup plain low-fat yogurt
8 small slices whole grain bread
2 tablespoons horseradish mustard
Fresh spinach or lettuce leaves
8 tomato slices

1

In a medium bowl combine the cottage cheese, carrot, sweet pepper or celery, and chives. Stir in the plain yogurt.

2

Spread one side of the bread slices with horseradish mustard; top the mustard on half of the bread slices with spinach or lettuce leaves. Spoon the cheese mixture onto spinach-lined bread slices. Top with tomato slices and remaining bread slices, mustard-sides down.

Nutrition Facts per serving: 248 calories, 7 g total fat, 12 mg cholesterol, 703 mg sodium, 32 g carbohydrate, 17 g protein.

GRILLED BRIE SANDWICHES WITH GREENS AND GARLIC

Another time, try this sophisticated grilled cheese sandwich with some watercress in place of half of the spinach.

Start to Finish: 20 minutes **Makes:** 4 servings

2 cloves garlic, minced

1 tablespoon olive oil or cooking oil

8 ounces torn fresh spinach (6 cups)

8 ounces cold Brie cheese, cut into
1/8-inch slices

8 slices firm-textured whole grain
bread

Margarine or butter

1

In a large skillet cook garlic in hot oil for 30 seconds. Add spinach. Cook over medium heat, tossing until spinach begins to wilt; remove from heat. Set aside.

2

Divide the cheese among 4 slices of the bread. Top with spinach-garlic mixture. Cover with remaining bread slices. Lightly spread the outside of each sandwich with margarine or butter.

3

In a large skillet cook 2 sandwiches over medium-low heat for 5 to 7 minutes or until golden. Turn sandwiches and cook about 2 minutes more or until sandwiches are golden and cheese melts. Transfer to a warm oven. Repeat with remaining sandwiches.

Nutrition Facts per serving: 405 calories, 27 g total fat, 57 mg cholesterol, 771 mg sodium, 25 g carbohydrate, 18 g protein.

GRILLED CHEESE-VEGGIE SANDWICHES

Grilled cheese sandwiches move uptown with a topping of cabbage, green pepper, and tomato.

Start to Finish: 20 minutes **Makes:** 4 servings

8 slices whole wheat bread
Nonstick cooking spray
8 thin slices reduced-fat cheddar
and/or Swiss cheese
(about 4 ounces total)

1 cup finely shredded cabbage
¼ cup chopped green sweet pepper
¼ cup chopped seeded tomato

1

Coat 1 side of each bread slice with the nonstick cooking spray. Place 2 bread slices, coated sides down, in a large nonstick skillet. Top each of the slices in the skillet with a slice of cheese.

2

Divide half of the cabbage, half of the sweet pepper, and half of the tomato evenly between the 2 bread slices. Top each with another slice of cheese. Place another bread slice on each sandwich, coated side up.

3

Cook sandwiches over medium heat for 3 to 4 minutes or until bread is toasted and cheese is melted, turning once. Keep sandwiches warm. Make 2 more sandwiches with remaining bread, remaining cheese, remaining cabbage, remaining sweet pepper, and remaining tomato.

Nutrition Facts per serving: 241 calories, 8 g total fat, 20 mg cholesterol, 500 mg sodium, 29 g carbohydrate, 14 g protein.

GRILLED EGG SANDWICHES

This unique sandwich is a cross between fried eggs and grilled cheese sandwiches.

Start to Finish: 20 minutes **Makes:** 2 servings

- 2 tablespoons mayonnaise or salad dressing
- 1 tablespoon Dijon-style mustard or brown mustard
- 4 slices English muffin bread or firm-textured white bread
- 1 tablespoon margarine or butter
- 2 eggs

- 4 to 6 fresh spinach leaves
- 1 small tomato, sliced
- 2 slices Swiss or American cheese (about 2 ounces total)
- 2 eggs
- 2 tablespoons milk
- 1 tablespoon margarine or butter

1
In a small bowl stir together mayonnaise or salad dressing and mustard. Spread the mustard mixture on 1 side of each bread slice. Set aside.

2
In a large skillet melt 1 tablespoon margarine or butter over medium heat. Break 2 eggs into skillet. Stir each egg gently with a fork to break up yolk. Cook for 3 to 4 minutes or until eggs are desired doneness, turning once.

3
Place each egg on mustard side of a bread slice. Layer the spinach, tomato, and cheese on eggs. Top with the remaining bread slices, mustard sides down.

4
In a shallow dish beat together 2 eggs and the milk. Carefully dip sandwiches into egg mixture, coating both sides. In the same skillet melt 1 tablespoon margarine or butter over medium heat. Add sandwiches. Cook about 4 minutes or until bread is golden brown, turning once.

Nutrition Facts per serving: 595 calories, 42 g total fat, 454 mg cholesterol, 692 mg sodium, 31 g carbohydrate, 24 g protein.

ITALIAN VEGETABLE MELT

A variety of fresh vegetables will work in this sandwich. Next time, try yellow summer squash in place of the zucchini and thin strips of fennel or kohlrabi in place of the sweet pepper.

Prep: 25 minutes **Broil:** 2 minutes **Makes:** 4 servings

2 individual French or Italian loaves
(each 6 to 7 inches long)

2 tablespoons bottled clear Italian
salad dressing

$\frac{1}{2}$ of a small onion, thinly sliced

$\frac{1}{2}$ of a small zucchini, halved
lengthwise and sliced

$\frac{1}{2}$ of a small green sweet pepper, cut
into thin strips

$\frac{1}{2}$ teaspoon bottled minced garlic or
1 clove garlic, minced

1 medium tomato, seeded and
chopped

$1\frac{1}{2}$ cups shredded provolone or
mozzarella cheese (6 ounces)

2 tablespoons grated Parmesan cheese

1

Split bread in half horizontally. Place halves on a baking sheet, cut sides up.

2

In a 10-inch skillet or wok heat the salad dressing. Add onion, zucchini, sweet pepper, and garlic. Stir-fry for 3 to 5 minutes or until crisp-tender. Stir in tomato. Sprinkle half of the provolone or mozzarella cheese on bread halves. Spoon vegetable mixture over cheese; sprinkle with remaining provolone or mozzarella and the Parmesan cheese.

3

Broil 3 to 4 inches from the heat about 2 minutes or until cheese melts.

Nutrition Facts per serving: 374 calories, 18 g total fat, 32 mg cholesterol, 836 mg sodium, 35 g carbohydrate, 18 g protein.

PEPPERY ARTICHOKE PITAS

Peppery arugula perks up this artichoke-and-bean pocket.

Start to Finish: 20 minutes **Makes:** 6 servings

1 15-ounce can Great Northern beans,
  rinsed and drained

1 13³/₄-to 14-ounce can artichoke
  hearts, drained and coarsely
  chopped

¹/₂ cup torn arugula or fresh spinach

¹/₄ cup bottled creamy garlic salad
  dressing

¹/₄ teaspoon cracked black pepper

3 pita bread rounds, halved crosswise

1

In a medium bowl combine Great Northern beans, artichoke hearts, arugula or spinach, salad dressing, and black pepper.

2

To serve, spoon bean mixture into pita bread halves.

Nutrition Facts per serving: 227 calories, 5 g total fat, 3 mg cholesterol, 269 mg sodium, 38 g carbohydrate, 10 g protein.

OPEN-FACE PORTOBELLO SANDWICHES

This stunning sandwich gives traditional stuffed mushrooms a new lease on life.

Start to Finish: 25 minutes **Makes:** 4 servings

1 medium tomato, chopped
2 teaspoons snipped fresh basil, thyme, and/or oregano
$\frac{1}{8}$ teaspoon salt
2 medium fresh portobello mushrooms (about 4 inches in diameter)
1 teaspoon balsamic vinegar or red wine vinegar

$\frac{1}{2}$ teaspoon olive oil
$\frac{1}{2}$ of a 12-inch Italian flat bread (focaccia) or $\frac{1}{2}$ of a 12-inch Italian bread shell (Boboli)
$\frac{1}{2}$ cup finely shredded Parmesan cheese

1

In a small bowl combine tomato, herb, and salt; set aside.

2

Remove and discard stems from mushrooms. In a small bowl combine the vinegar and oil; gently brush over mushrooms. Place mushrooms on the unheated rack of the broiler pan. Broil 4 to 5 inches from the heat for 6 to 8 minutes or just until mushrooms are tender, turning once halfway through broiling. Drain mushrooms on paper towels. Thinly slice mushrooms; set aside.

3

Place the bread on a baking sheet. Broil for 2 to 3 minutes or until bread is heated through. Arrange the mushroom slices and tomato mixture on top of bread. Sprinkle with Parmesan cheese.

Nutrition Facts per serving: 205 calories, 7 g total fat, 10 mg cholesterol, 316 mg sodium, 27 g carbohydrate, 11 g protein.

RICE 'N' BEAN TOSTADOS

Purchase packaged torn mixed salad greens to make these tostados extra easy.

Start to Finish: 25 minutes **Makes:** 4 servings

1½ cups water
1½ cups quick-cooking brown rice
1 medium onion, chopped
1 15-ounce can chili beans with chili
    gravy
1 8-ounce can whole kernel corn,
    drained

4 9- to 10-inch flour tortillas
3 cups torn mixed salad greens
½ cup shredded cheddar cheese
    (2 ounces)
¼ cup dairy sour cream
1 medium tomato, chopped

1

In a large saucepan bring the water to boiling. Stir in rice and onion. Return to boiling; reduce heat. Cover and simmer for 5 minutes. Remove from heat. Stir. Cover and let stand for 5 minutes. Stir undrained chili beans and drained corn into rice mixture. Heat through.

2

Meanwhile, place tortillas on a large baking sheet, overlapping as necessary. Bake in a 400°F oven about 10 minutes or until tortillas begin to brown around the edges.

3

To serve, place each tortilla on a dinner plate. Top tortillas with salad greens and the rice-bean mixture. Sprinkle with cheddar cheese. Top with sour cream and chopped tomato.

Nutrition Facts per serving: 512 calories, 14 g total fat, 21 mg cholesterol, 735 mg sodium, 81 g carbohydrate, 19 g protein.

ZUCCHINI, CORN, AND POTATO TACOS

Zucchini, carrots, potato, and corn join forces with tofu and cheese to make these hefty tacos as satisfying as they are colorful.

Start to Finish: 30 minutes **Makes:** 6 servings

1 medium potato, cut into $\frac{1}{2}$-inch cubes (1 cup)

2 medium carrots, chopped

12 taco shells

$\frac{1}{2}$ cup chopped onion

1 clove garlic, minced

1 tablespoon olive oil or cooking oil

1 small zucchini, cut into thin, bite-size strips (about 1$\frac{1}{4}$ cups)

1 cup loose-pack frozen whole kernel corn

1 tablespoon chili powder

$\frac{1}{2}$ teaspoon salt

$\frac{1}{8}$ teaspoon ground black pepper

8 ounces firm tofu (fresh bean curd), cut into $\frac{1}{2}$-inch cubes

1 cup shredded cheddar and/or Monterey Jack cheese (4 ounces)

Bottled salsa (optional)

Sliced green onions (optional)

Dairy sour cream (optional)

Avocado slices (optional)

1

In a covered medium saucepan cook the potato and carrots in a small amount of boiling water for 7 to 8 minutes or just until tender; drain and set aside. If desired, heat taco shells according to package directions.

2

Meanwhile, in a large skillet cook and stir onion and garlic in hot oil over medium-high heat for 2 minutes. Add zucchini and corn; cook and stir for 3 minutes more. Add chili powder, salt, and pepper; cook and stir for 1 minute more. Gently stir in the potato mixture and tofu; heat through.

3

To serve, fill the taco shells with the vegetable-tofu mixture. Sprinkle with cheese. If desired, serve with salsa, green onions, sour cream, and/or avocado.

Nutrition Facts per serving: 315 calories, 16 g total fat, 20 mg cholesterol, 438 mg sodium, 34 g carbohydrate, 11 g protein.

FRESH TOMATO PIZZA WITH PESTO

This easy six-ingredient pizza is a fantastic way to help use up summer's bumper crop of tomatoes.

Prep: 15 minutes **Bake:** 10 minutes **Makes:** 4 servings

$^1/_2$ cup purchased pesto
1 16-ounce Italian bread shell
   (Boboli)
3 medium ripe tomatoes, thinly sliced
   Freshly ground black pepper

1 2$^1/_4$-ounce can sliced pitted ripe
   olives, drained
2 cups shredded Monterey Jack or
   mozzarella cheese (8 ounces)

1

Spread pesto evenly over bread shell. Place on a large pizza pan or a large baking sheet. Arrange tomato slices on top. Season with pepper. Sprinkle with olives. Sprinkle with cheese.

2

Bake in a 425°F oven for 10 to 15 minutes or until cheese melts and tomatoes are warm. To serve, cut into wedges.

Nutrition Facts per serving: 776 calories, 48 g total fat, 60 mg cholesterol, 1,265 mg sodium, 60 g carbohydrate, 32 g protein.

GRILLED SICILIAN-STYLE PIZZA

*For an authentic finish to this meatless meal, serve biscotti and a
sweet dessert wine or cappuccino for dessert.*

Prep: 20 minutes **Grill:** 8 minutes **Makes:** 4 servings

1 16-ounce Italian bread shell
   (Boboli)
2 plum tomatoes, thinly sliced
1 large yellow or red tomato, thinly
   sliced
4 ounces fresh mozzarella or buffalo
   mozzarella cheese, thinly sliced

$\frac{1}{3}$ cup halved pitted kalamata olives or
   ripe olives
1 tablespoon olive oil
1 cup coarsely chopped escarole or
   curly endive
$\frac{1}{4}$ cup shredded Romano or Parmesan
   cheese (1 ounce)
   Freshly ground black pepper

1

Top bread shell with plum tomatoes, yellow or red tomatoes, mozzarella cheese, and olives. Drizzle oil over all. Fold a 24×18-inch piece of heavy foil in half lengthwise. Place pizza on foil, turning edges of foil up to edge of pizza.

2

In a grill with a cover arrange medium-hot coals around edge of the grill. Test for medium heat over center of the grill. Place pizza on the grill rack in center of grill. Cover and grill about 8 minutes or until pizza is heated through, topping with escarole or endive for the last 2 minutes of grilling.

3

To serve, sprinkle cheese and pepper over pizza.

Nutrition Facts per serving: 459 calories, 19 g total fat, 26 mg cholesterol, 893 mg sodium, 54 g carbohydrate, 24 g protein.

NUTTY ENDIVE PIZZA WITH TWO CHEESES

Walnut oil boosts the flavor of the nuts in this sophisticated pizza.

Prep: 15 minutes **Bake:** 10 minutes **Makes:** 4 servings

1 small red onion, chopped
2 cloves garlic, minced
1 tablespoon walnut oil or olive oil
4 cups torn curly endive or fresh
   spinach
¼ teaspoon crushed red pepper

1 16-ounce Italian bread shell (Boboli)
1 cup shredded Swiss cheese (4 ounces)
¼ cup pine nuts or coarsely chopped
   walnuts, toasted
1 cup shredded Colby cheese (4 ounces)

1

In a medium skillet cook red onion and garlic in hot oil until tender. Add endive or spinach and crushed red pepper. Cover and cook over low heat for 2 minutes.

2

Place bread shell on a 12-inch pizza pan or large baking sheet. Sprinkle Swiss cheese evenly over bread shell. Top with endive mixture and toasted nuts. Sprinkle Colby cheese over the top. Bake in a 425°F oven about 10 minutes or until cheese melts.

3

To serve, cut pizza into wedges.

Nutrition Facts per serving: 616 calories, 32 g total fat, 58 mg cholesterol, 878 mg sodium, 56 g carbohydrate, 31 g protein.

PORTOBELLO PIZZAS

*Portobello mushrooms are meaty, super-size brown mushrooms with caps
that are 3 or more inches across.*

Prep: 15 minutes **Grill:** 8 minutes **Makes:** 4 servings

4 portobello mushrooms
Olive oil
Salt
Ground black pepper

1 4-ounce round Brie cheese, thinly
   sliced
1 small tomato, cut up
¼ cup firmly packed arugula leaves

1

Clean and remove the stems from mushrooms. Discard stems. Brush both sides of the mushroom caps
with oil. Sprinkle with salt and pepper.

2

In a grill with a cover arrange medium-hot coals around the edge of the grill. Test for medium heat
over center of the grill. Place mushrooms, rounded sides down, on the grill rack in center of the grill.
Cover and grill for 8 to 10 minutes or until mushrooms are tender and hot, turning once halfway
through grilling. (Or arrange mushrooms, rounded sides down, on a baking sheet. Bake in a 400°F oven
for 8 to 10 minutes, turning once halfway through baking.)

3

To serve, drizzle mushrooms with a little more oil. Top with cheese, tomato, and arugula.

Nutrition Facts per serving: 181 calories, 16 g total fat, 28 mg cholesterol, 256 mg sodium, 5 g carbohydrate, 10 g protein.

VEGETABLE BREAKFAST PIZZA

For brunch, serve this morning special with a fruit compote and your favorite flavored coffee or tea.

Prep: 25 minutes **Bake:** 8 minutes **Makes:** 6 to 8 servings

Nonstick cooking spray
1½ cups loose-pack frozen diced hash brown potatoes or country-style hash brown potatoes with skin, thawed
1 cup sliced fresh mushrooms
½ cup shredded carrot
½ cup shredded zucchini
¼ cup chopped onion

1 cup refrigerated or frozen egg product, thawed, or 4 eggs
¼ cup fat-free milk
1 16-ounce Italian bread shell (Boboli)
½ cup shredded reduced-fat mozzarella cheese (2 ounces)
½ cup chopped tomato

1

Coat an unheated large skillet with nonstick cooking spray. Preheat over medium heat. Add the potatoes, mushrooms, carrot, zucchini, and onion; cook and stir about 3 minutes or until vegetables are tender.

2

In a small bowl stir together egg product or eggs and milk. Pour over vegetables. Cook, without stirring, until mixture begins to set on the bottom and around the edge. Using a spatula or a large spoon, lift and fold the partially cooked egg mixture so the uncooked portion flows underneath. Continue cooking and folding about 4 minutes or until egg product is cooked through but is still glossy and moist. Remove from heat.

3

To assemble pizza, place the Italian bread shell on a 12-inch pizza pan or a large baking sheet. Sprinkle with half of the cheese. Top with the egg mixture, tomato, and remaining cheese. Bake in a 375°F oven for 8 to 10 minutes or until cheese is melted.

4

To serve, cut into wedges.

Nutrition Facts per serving: 300 calories, 6 g total fat, 4 mg cholesterol, 577 mg sodium, 47 g carbohydrate, 18 g protein.

INDEX

Emergency Substitutions

It you don't have:	Substitute:
Bacon, 1 slice, crisp-cooked, crumbled	1 tablespoon cooked bacon pieces
Baking powder, 1 teaspoon	½ teaspoon cream of tartar plus ¼ teaspoon baking soda
Balsamic vinegar, 1 tablespoon	1 tablespoon cider vinegar or red wine vinegar plus ½ teaspoon sugar
Bread crumbs, fine dry, ¼ cup	¾ cup soft bread crumbs, or ¼ cup cracker crumbs, or ¼ cup cornflake crumbs
Broth, beef or chicken, 1 cup	1 teaspoon or 1 cube instant beef or chicken bouillon plus 1 cup hot water
Butter, 1 cup	1 cup shortening plus ¼ teaspoon salt, if desired
Buttermilk, 1 cup	1 tablespoon lemon juice or vinegar plus enough milk to make 1 cup (let stand 5 minutes before using) or 1 cup plain yogurt
Chocolate, semisweet, 1 ounce	3 tablespoons semisweet chocolate pieces, or 1 ounce unsweetened chocolate plus 1 tablespoon granulated sugar, or 1 tablespoon unsweetened cocoa powder plus 2 teaspoons sugar and 2 teaspoons shortening
Chocolate, sweet baking, 4 ounces	¼ cup unsweetened cocoa powder plus ⅓ cup granulated sugar and 3 tablespoons shortening
Chocolate, unsweetened, 1 ounce	3 tablespoons unsweetened cocoa powder plus 1 tablespoon cooking oil or shortening, melted
Cornstarch, 1 tablespoon (for thickening)	2 tablespoons all-purpose flour
Corn syrup (light), 1 cup	1 cup granulated sugar plus ¼ cup water
Egg, 1 whole	2 egg whites, or 2 egg yolks, or ¼ cup refrigerated or frozen egg product, thawed
Flour, cake, 1 cup	1 cup minus 2 tablespoons all-purpose flour
Flour, self-rising, 1 cup	1 cup all-purpose flour plus 1 teaspoon baking powder, ½ teaspoon salt, and ¼ teaspoon baking soda
Garlic, 1 clove	½ teaspoon bottled minced garlic or ⅛ teaspoon garlic powder
Ginger, grated fresh, 1 teaspoon	¼ teaspoon ground ginger
Half-and-half or light cream, 1 cup	1 tablespoon melted butter or margarine plus enough whole milk to make 1 cup
Molasses, 1 cup	1 cup honey
Mustard, dry, 1 teaspoon	1 tablespoon prepared (in cooked mixtures)
Mustard, prepared, 1 tablespoon	½ teaspoon dry mustard plus 2 teaspoons vinegar
Onion, chopped, ½ cup	2 tablespoons dried minced onion or ½ teaspoon onion powder
Sour cream, dairy, 1 cup	1 cup plain yogurt
Sugar, granulated, 1 cup	1 cup packed brown sugar or 2 cups sifted powdered sugar
Sugar, brown, 1 cup packed	1 cup granulated sugar plus 2 tablespoons molasses
Tomato juice, 1 cup	½ cup tomato sauce plus ½ cup water
Tomato sauce, 2 cups	¾ cup tomato paste plus 1 cup water
Vanilla bean, 1 whole	2 teaspoons vanilla extract
Wine, red, 1 cup	1 cup beef or chicken broth in savory recipes; cranberry juice in desserts
Wine, white, 1 cup	1 cup chicken broth in savory recipes; apple juice or white grape juice in desserts
Yeast, active dry, 1 package	about 2¼ teaspoons active dry yeast

Seasonings

Apple pie spice, 1 teaspoon	½ teaspoon ground cinnamon plus ¼ teaspoon ground nutmeg, ⅛ teaspoon ground allspice, and dash ground cloves or ginger
Cajun seasoning, 1 tablespoon	½ teaspoon white pepper, ½ teaspoon garlic powder, ½ teaspoon onion powder, ½ teaspoon ground red pepper, ½ teaspoon paprika, and ½ teaspoon ground black pepper
Herbs, snipped fresh, 1 tablespoon	½ to 1 teaspoon dried herb, crushed, or ½ teaspoon ground herb
Poultry seasoning, 1 teaspoon	¾ teaspoon dried sage, crushed, plus ¼ teaspoon dried thyme or marjoram, crushed
Pumpkin pie spice, 1 teaspoon	½ teaspoon ground cinnamon plus ¼ teaspoon ground ginger, ¼ teaspoon ground allspice, and ⅛ teaspoon ground nutmeg

Metric Information

The charts on this page provide a guide for converting measurements from the U.S. customary system, which is used throughout this book, to the metric system.

Product Differences

Most of the ingredients called for in the recipes in this book are available in most countries. However, some are known by different names. Here are some common American ingredients and their possible counterparts:

- Sugar (white) is granulated, fine granulated, or castor sugar.
- Powdered sugar is icing sugar.
- All-purpose flour is enriched, bleached or unbleached, white household flour. When self-rising flour is used in place of all-purpose flour in a recipe that calls for leavening, omit the leavening agent (baking soda or baking powder) and salt.
- Light-colored corn syrup is golden syrup.
- Cornstarch is cornflour.
- Baking soda is bicarbonate of soda.
- Vanilla or vanilla extract is vanilla essence.
- Green, red, or yellow sweet peppers are capsicums or bell peppers.
- Golden raisins are sultanas.

Volume and Weight

The United States traditionally uses cup measures for liquid and solid ingredients. The chart below shows the approximate imperial and metric equivalents. If you are accustomed to weighing solid ingredients, the following approximate equivalents will be helpful.

- 1 cup butter, castor sugar, or rice = 8 ounces = ½ pound = 250 grams
- 1 cup flour = 4 ounces = ¼ pound = 125 grams
- 1 cup icing sugar = 5 ounces = 150 grams

Canadian and U.S. volume for a cup measure is 8 fluid ounces (237 ml), but the standard metric equivalent is 250 ml.

1 British imperial cup is 10 fluid ounces.

In Australia, 1 tablespoon equals 20 ml, and there are 4 teaspoons in the Australian tablespoon.

Spoon measures are used for smaller amounts of ingredients. Although the size of the tablespoon varies slightly in different countries, for practical purposes and for recipes in this book, a straight substitution is all that's necessary. Measurements made using cups or spoons always should be level unless stated otherwise.

Common Weight Range Replacements

Imperial / U.S.	Metric
½ ounce	15 g
1 ounce	25 g or 30 g
4 ounces (¼ pound)	115 g or 125 g
8 ounces (½ pound)	225 g or 250 g
16 ounces (1 pound)	450 g or 500 g
1¼ pounds	625 g
1½ pounds	750 g
2 pounds or 2¼ pounds	1,000 g or 1 Kg

Oven Temperature Equivalents

Fahrenheit Setting	Celsius Setting*	Gas Setting
300°F	150°C	Gas Mark 2 (very low)
325°F	160°C	Gas Mark 3 (low)
350°F	180°C	Gas Mark 4 (moderate)
375°F	190°C	Gas Mark 5 (moderate)
400°F	200°C	Gas Mark 6 (hot)
425°F	220°C	Gas Mark 7 (hot)
450°F	230°C	Gas Mark 8 (very hot)
475°F	240°C	Gas Mark 9 (very hot)
500°F	260°C	Gas Mark 10 (extremely hot)
Broil	Broil	Grill

*Electric and gas ovens may be calibrated using celsius. However, for an electric oven, increase celsius setting 10 to 20 degrees when cooking above 160°C. For convection or forced air ovens (gas or electric), lower the temperature setting 25°F/10°C when cooking at all heat levels.

Baking Pan Sizes

Imperial / U.S.	Metric
9×1½-inch round cake pan	22- or 23×4-cm (1.5 L)
9×1½-inch pie plate	22- or 23×4-cm (1 L)
8×8×2-inch square cake pan	20×5-cm (2 L)
9×9×2-inch square cake pan	22- or 23×4.5-cm (2.5 L)
11×7×1½-inch baking pan	28×17×4-cm (2 L)
2-quart rectangular baking pan	30×19×4.5-cm (3 L)
13×9×2-inch baking pan	34×22×4.5-cm (3.5 L)
15×10×1-inch jelly roll pan	40×25×2-cm
9×5×3-inch loaf pan	23×13×8-cm (2 L)
2-quart casserole	2 L

U.S. / Standard Metric Equivalents

⅛ teaspoon = 0.5 ml	
¼ teaspoon = 1 ml	
½ teaspoon = 2 ml	
1 teaspoon = 5 ml	
1 tablespoon = 15 ml	
2 tablespoons = 25 ml	
¼ cup = 2 fluid ounces = 50 ml	
⅓ cup = 3 fluid ounces = 75 ml	
½ cup = 4 fluid ounces = 125 ml	
⅔ cup = 5 fluid ounces = 150 ml	
¾ cup = 6 fluid ounces = 175 ml	
1 cup = 8 fluid ounces = 250 ml	
2 cups = 1 pint = 500 ml	
1 quart = 1 litre	